ROBERT REDFORD
and the
AMERICAN WEST

ROBERT REDFORD
and the
AMERICAN WEST

A critical essay by
ELISA LEONELLI

To order additional copies of this book, contact:
Xlibris Corporation
1-888-795-4274
www.Xlibris.com
Orders@Xlibris.com
38683

CONTENTS

PREFACE

My love affair with the movies

My love affair with the movies began when I was a child growing up in Italy in the 1950s. My permissive mother Dina would allow me to walk to the local cinema by myself in the afternoons, or my father Enzo, an avid moviegoer, would take me along. In elementary school I loved comedies with Dean Martin and Jerry Lewis, such as *Artists and Models* (1955), musicals such as *Brigadoon* (1954), science fiction such as *20,000 Leagues Under the Sea* (1954) based on the novel by a beloved author, Jules Verne (I was also a voracious reader). My favorite actors were Tony Curtis in *Trapeze* (1956), Rock Hudson in *Pillow Talk* (1959) with Doris Day, Tony Perkins in *Psycho* (1960) by Alfred Hitchcock. This was before I saw Sean Connery in *From Russia with Love* (1963), when he became and remained my favorite actor of all time. I had stopped going to the movies with my father by then, after he had suddenly realized one day that I was no longer a child, when he had to buy two adult admissions for *The Diary of Anne Frank* (1959). At age 14 I had started seeing films on Saturday afternoons with my first boyfriend, a basketball player nicknamed "Pesce" for his fish-like weaving on the court; while having a secret crush on Jean-Paul Belmondo in *Breathless* (1959). At age 16 I left the Catholic Church, when I discovered sex with my second boyfriend, and I began considering myself a politically engaged intellectual. That was the time of the great Italian cinema by Pier Paolo Pasolini and Michelangelo Antonioni—I decided I wanted to become a photographer after seeing *Blow-up* (1966)—but our god was Jean-Luc Godard; he truly revolutionized cinema.

It was in this atmosphere that I started college, at 17, studying Liberal Arts at the University of Bologna; and by the time I became disillusioned with the student movement in 1969, I had to decide what I was going to do with my life. So I thought, why not work in the movies, it sounded interesting and fun; perhaps I could become an underground filmmaker like Stan Brackage—by then the psychedelic revolution had been coloring our vision with rainbows. Unfortunately there were no film studies departments in Italian universities yet (the first one would start in the fall of 1970), so I had to find a professor willing to help me create my own curriculum. Luciano Anceschi, who taught Aesthetics, consented and put me on a film study regimen that included Siegfried Kracauer's *From Caligari to Hitler* (1947); he suggested I write a thesis about the work of French novelist and filmmaker Alain Robbe-Grillet—founder of the *nouveau roman*, he had written the screenplay for *Last Year at Marienbad* (1962) by Alain Resnais and directed *Trans-Europe Express* (1966) with Jean-Louis Trintignant.

Armed with these impressive credentials, I moved to Rome, planning to attend the only film school in Italy, Centro Sperimentale di Cinematografia. The professors welcomed me warmly, and I was able to work on some of the student films, however bureaucracy would not allow me to officially register until nearly two years later. Meanwhile I was offered a position as film critic at the Pesaro film festival, where I worked with Adriano Aprá; our job was to study each of the chosen films at the moviola and write frame-by-frame descriptions. This is how I befriended and worked with up-and-coming filmmakers, such as Peter Del Monte. I also met a crazy American, Stuart Birnbaum, a recent graduate of USC Film School, who was a student observer on Federico Fellini's *Roma*. We fell in love and I accepted his invitation to join him in New York; on my first night in America we went to see *Diamonds are Forever* (1971). The man I would later marry was also a film lover and we would get excited together watching Hitchcok's films at the Vagabond (we had moved to Hollywood in 1973); my favorites were *Vertigo* (1958), *Rear Window* (1954), *Suspicion* (1941), *Rebecca* (1940).

A big revolution had happened in my filmgoing: I was finally able to hear the original English dialogue, rather than the version dubbed in Italian that was and still is the custom in my country. This added the immense pleasure of actually hearing the actors give their performances; and it's now something I could never do without again (that is one of the many reason I never moved back to Italy.)

Professionally I eventually decided to become a still photographer, not a filmmaker, because I realized I would be able to work alone, with the camera almost a part of my body, and create my own images more freely. I started writing for magazines to tell the stories of my pictures. I traveled around the world with my Nikons—to China, India, Peru, Brazil, Jamaica—exploring other cultures, bringing back only colorful slides as souvenirs. When I was in Los Angeles, I would photograph movie stars—as well as performance artists such as the Kipper Kids—at their home, on location or in my studio; and I would also interview them. I had become a member of ASMP, American Society of Media Photographers, MPAA, Motion Picture Association, HFPA, Hollywood Foreign Press. In 1985 I was afflicted by back problems that caused me to slow down my work as a photographer and increase my writing; eventually I gave up photography all together (1990).

By then I had become focused on writing about movies full time, as the Los Angeles correspondent for the Italian film monthly *Ciak* (since 1987) and Film Editor for *Venice*, the Los Angeles Arts and Entertainment magazine (since 1989). And I was happy because not only was I seeing every single movie made in Hollywood, but I had a chance to talk to the people who actually made them—the actors, the directors—and ask them any questions I wanted. I spoke with exciting actors like Russell Crowe and Meryl Streep, thoughtful directors like Michael Apted and Bruce Beresford, and countless others. What I would always highlight in my articles were the themes that had some relevance to our society, the changing mores in marriage and child rearing, the political implications. Starting in the late sixties and more frequently since the nineties, I also traveled to film festivals around the world—from Telluride to Zanzibar—to meet filmmakers of different nationalities and learn about their cultures. That's when I felt the desire to study cinema from an academic standpoint, to finally walk on the green campus of an American university; and I chose USC, George Lucas Alma Mater.

Marsha Kinder, director of the Critical Studies Department, welcomed me and lead me through studies of the film theories that had been developed in the previous few decades. I had the great pleasure of studying silent cinema with Yuri Tsivian, a Russian professor who was enchanted to find out that in my youth I had played Lulu in an underground version of Pabst's masterpiece, *Pandora's Box* (1928) with Louise Brooks (*Lulu*, directed by Ronald Chase, was presented at Filmex in 1978). One of the first assignments I received from Steve Hanson, director of the Cinema Library, was to write a book proposal. That's when I first had the idea of writing about Robert Redford's work as a director, because I had been exceedingly impressed by his *A River Runs Through It*, which I had seen in Toronto, when I also interviewed him for the first time for *Venice* magazine. For another class I would create a multi-media study of that film; then I asked my thesis advisor, Professor Richard Jewell, if Redford would be an acceptable subject of critical study. He said yes, but I needed a focus; so I traveled to the Sundance labs (June 1994), stayed in that tranquil resort, and that's when it hit me: the American West. That could be the through line of Redford's work as an actor, director and founder of the Sundance Institute. So I wrote my thesis and earned my Master's Degree (1997), but that was before Redford's directed *The Horse Whisperer,* and I always wanted to update my study to include that important film. I didn't get around to it until recently—I was busy raising a teenage daughter who's now in college (Samantha Lyon is studying Political Science and International Relations at Smith, class of 2008); but here it is.

I would like to thank all the people mentioned above for encouraging my love of cinema, and my friend Christopher Lanier, my most frequent filmgoing companion of the last twenty-five years, for his help as a sounding board on this book.

INTRODUCTION

Outline and Methodology

Robert Redford is known all over the world as one of the biggest movie stars of Hollywood cinema since the 1970s, after the success of films like *Butch Cassidy and the Sundance Kid* (1969) and *The Sting* (1973), where he was paired with Paul Newman, *The Way We Were* (1973) with Barbra Streisand and *All the President's Men* (1976) with Dustin Hoffmann. He continued to be a bankable star in the 1980s, in films like *The Natural* (1984) with Glenn Close and *Out of Africa* (1985) with Meryl Streep, and the 1990s in *Indecent Proposal* (1992) with Demi Moore and *Up Close and Personal* (1996) with Michelle Pfeiffer, until the present, in *Spy Games* (2001) with Brad Pitt.

As soon as he gained power in the industry, Redford began to produce his own films, such as *The Candidate* (1972) by Michael Ritchie and *All the President's Men* (1976) by Alan Pakula, then to direct, starting with *Ordinary People* (1980) which earned him an Oscar as Best Director, continuing with *The Milagro Beanfield War* (1986), *A River Runs Through It* (1992), *Quiz Show* (1994), *The Horse Whisperer* (1998) and *The Legend of Bagger Vance* (2000).

Redford is a strong supporter of independent films, since founding the Sundance Institute in 1981 and the Sundance Film Festival in 1985, an event that has become increasingly important in bringing to the attention of the public interesting films from *Sex, Lies and Videotape* (1989) to *Little Miss Sunshine* (2006). He has been extremely vocal in his environmental activism since the 1970s and recently in his opposition to the Bush administration's policies.

Redford's contributions to the history of cinema and his iconic status in American culture make him a worthy subject for a critical study. For this book I have chosen to outline how Redford's work can be interpreted as emblematic of the best values of the American West, in a time when the legacy of violence born on the frontier has come under question.

The unique American mythology of the West was spread all over the world through cinema and television, particularly since the 1950s, after the US military involvement during World War II. "No genre has retained more continuous popularity than the Western; nor is any genre more involved with fundamental American beliefs about individualism and social progress. Many American and European film scholars have approached the Western as a peculiarly American cultural form."[1] Every generation of filmmakers has employed the familiar themes of the Western to express their concerns about the present; Redford began his film career by portraying some flawed western heroes in counter-culture Westerns of the late 1960s that questioned American ideals during the Vietnam War.

He played a dangerous but charming outlaw in the buddy film *Butch Cassidy and the Sundance Kid* (1969) written by William Goldman and directed by George Roy Hill, which made him famous. He was a sheriff chasing a fugitive Indian in *Tell Them Willie Boy is Here* (1968) written and directed by Abraham Polonsky and a laconic mountain man challenged by Indian braves in *Jeremiah Johnson* (1972) directed by Sydney Pollack. Fascinated by the lifestyle of the outlaws as true representatives of the western free spirit, he accepted an offer from National Geographic to take a trip on horseback retracing their steps through Montana, Utah and Arizona, and wrote the text for the picture book *The Outlaw Trail* (1978). He then played a rodeo cowboy in *The Electric Horseman* (1979) with Jane Fonda, which is not strictly a Western—director Sydney Pollack calls it a romantic comedy—but deals with the connection between a cowboy and his horse as a symbol of the individual freedom that has been lost in a modern society dominated by greed and an invasive media. Redford would explore a similar subject, the spiritual centeredness of a Montana rancher with a gift for talking to horses, in his film as a director, *The Horse Whisperer* (1998).

Recently he played an older, embittered rancher looking for forgiveness in *An Unfinished Life* (2005) directed by Lasse Hallström.

Through these different portrayals of iconic western characters on the big screen, Redford has become a physical representative of the enduring values of the real American West, in more subversive ways than the traditional western heroes of classical cinema. He accomplished this in part by embracing the spiritual values of the indigenous American Indian culture. He demonstrated his interest in the plight of modern Indians by producing several films based on the novels by Tony Hillerman, from *The Dark Wind* (1990) to *A Thief of Time* (2004), and the documentary about Leonard Peltier, *Incident at Oglala* (1992).

The creation of the Sundance ski resort and the Sundance Institute proved Redford's commitment to preserve the natural beauty of the American West, which would inspire his environmental activism. His second film as director, *The Milagro Beanfield War* (1986), celebrated the victory of Southwest farmers who cultivate the land against greedy developers who exploit the land. *A River Runs through It* (1992) illustrated his nostalgia for the unspoiled western landscape and the mystical relationship between man and nature in 1920s Montana. Other films Redford directed don't have to do specifically with the West, but are considered here because they deal with essential elements of the American character, such as the disillusionment with American ideals in *Quiz Show* (1994) and the mythology of sports in *The Legend of Bagger Vance* (2000).

As a European woman who became politically aware during the cultural revolution of the late 1960s and the feminist movement of the early 1970s, I recognize in Robert Redford, who came of age in post-war America during the repressive 1950s and rebelled against his country's conformism, a questioning of the conservative American male values represented in films by older western heroes like John Wayne and in politics by Ronald Reagan and George W. Bush. And I admire his forward-thinking efforts in defense of the environment and his progressive political ideas that put more faith in grass-root movements than in professional politicians.

For this study I employ a functional methodology that combines my practical experience as a journalist with my theoretical background as a film scholar. In my opinion, in examining a work of art such as a film, critics should take into consideration the actual intentions of the authors; mainly the directors, the actors and the screenwriters. Therefore I include in my textual analysis of the films extensive quotes from interviews I personally conducted with such authors, and from other published articles. I borrow concepts from *auteur* theory,[2] I make reference to recent theoretical texts about the history of the West and the western genre, and offer comparisons with other modern Westerns, to underline certain themes and preoccupations that Redford shares with his contemporaries.

After the Western had "apparently died" in the 1970s, according to many critics, the success of *Dances with Wolves* (1990) by Kevin Costner and *Unforgiven* (1992) by Clint Eastwood encouraged the production of a number of Westerns in the mid-1990s. Lately the genre is not as visible on the big screen, but continues to have a healthy life on television in such works as *Deadwood* (2003-2007), *Into the West* (2005) by Steven Spielberg and *Broken Trail* (2006) by Walter Hill. These contemporary Westerns offer a revisionist interpretation of traditional themes and reflect in the popular media the theories of New Western historians, such as Patricia Limerick and Richard White. In recent years there has been more attention paid to the plight of the Indians as victims of the white man's conquest of the West, to the contribution of ethnic minorities like Blacks and Hispanics in the settling of the West, to the role of pioneer women, and to the legacy of violence that the Western represents in American culture.

To demonstrate the continuity as well as the changes in the western film genre, and connect it to its literary and historical roots, I quote from books such as *Showdown. Confronting Modern America in the Western Film* (1980) by John Lenihan, *The Western Hero in Film and Television* (1982) by Rita Parks, *The Six Guns Mystique* (1984) by John Cawelti, *A Certain Tendency of the Hollywood Cinema, 1930-1980* (1985) by Robert Ray, *The Legacy of Conquest: the Unbroken Past of the American West* (1987) by Patricia Nelson Limerick, *Playing Cowboys. Low Culture and High Art in the Western (1991)* by Robert Murray Davis, *Gunfighter Nation: The Myth of the Frontier in Twentieth Century America* (1992) by Richard Slotkin, *West of Everything: The inner life of Westerns* (1992) by Jane Tompkins, *The Crowded Prairie: American National Identity in the Hollywood Western*

(1997) by Michael Coyne, *Invisible Natives: Myth & Identity in the American Western* (2002) by Armando José Prats.

Using these methods, I highlight the western themes running through Robert Redford's work: the problematic relationship between the white man on the frontier and the Indians, the role of women and family as a civilizing influence on the violent western hero, the youthful fascination with legendary outlaws, the destructive influence of greedy developers on the preservation of natural resources, and the nostalgia for a spiritual connection between mankind and nature. I show that Redford believes in traditional historical and literary American values and criticizes the trivializing effect of the modern media and the commercial mentality that dominates Hollywood films, that his political views are progressive in his defense of the environment and his opposition to the policies of the current administration. The choices that Redford has made throughout his career, as an actor, producer, director, and founder of Sundance, demonstrate the thoughtful and coherent intentions of an artist who has consistently dealt with issues that he felt were important in our society.

1. TELL THEM WILLIE BOY IS HERE

Indians are people.

In *Tell Them Willie Boy is Here* (1969) Redford represents a new type of western hero compared to the traditional lawman of classic Westerns, and his victory over the Indian outlaw is meaningless; it does not serve the purpose of restoring the social order in the town, as in movies like *Shane* (1952) or *My Darling Clementine* (1946). "Robert Warshow, in his celebrated essay on the Western," says Lenihan, "defines the Western in terms of its hero, a lone man of honor, whose six-gun, tempered with his sense of justice and rectitude, wins the West on behalf of society."[1] In the interpretation of writer-director Abraham Polonsky, the Indian is also a hero, equal to the white man, and the manhunt against him is blown out of proportion by external political causes. This situates the film among the pro-Indian Westerns produced in a post-war America that was becoming more aware of racial prejudice. "From the hopeful integrationist sentiment of *Broken Arrow* (1950) to the despairing indictment of *Little Big Man* (1970), the Western's increasing emphasis on frontier discrimination against the Indian paralleled growing contemporary sensitivity about social injustice towards blacks."[2]

Although his contribution to this film was only that of an actor, Redford could feel attuned to this kind of representation, because of the admiration and respect for the Indians that he would demonstrate in his later work.

In *Tell Them Willie Boy is Here* Redford plays Sheriff Christopher Cooper, nicknamed "Coop" just like Gary Cooper, the prototypical western hero of

American cinema, but he represents a different kind of hero. Under-sheriff of Banning, California, he's a reluctant lawman who performs the duties of his job without much conviction. He's introduced when arriving late at a fiesta at the Morongo Reservation, gingerly eating a piece of fruit on horseback, after having been summoned by superintendent Elizabeth Arnold (Susan Clark) to arrest white men selling liquor to "her" Indians. Later that night, when he receives a complaint about a drunken Indian—that same Willie Boy who had bought a bottle of whiskey earlier—he simply walks over to the pool hall and tells everybody to go home. He will later regret not having picked up the Indian when he had the chance, but, as he tells Liz, "I was hungry for you." Shortly after that we see Coop knocking at the door of this sophisticated woman from the East for one of their secret love encounters.

Redford was chosen to portray this new type of disenchanted hero with a weakness for women, partly because he was a young actor who didn't have a baggage of previous Western performances. In 1968 he was not yet a star and he was last on a list of actors presented by Universal's Jennings Lang to writer-director Abraham Polonsky. Warren Beatty was first on the list, after starring in *Bonnie and Clyde* the year before. In fact, Beatty was also offered the role of Sundance in *Butch Cassidy and the Sundance Kid*, after Steve McQueen turned it down and Marlon Brando was nowhere to be found. But director George Roy Hill was convinced Redford was the right guy—after having seen footage from *Tell Them Willie Boy is Here*—and asked Paul Newman and screenwriter William Goldman to back him up (Hill also hired the same cinematographer, Conrad Hall, because he liked the stark look of his western films). The release of *Tell Them Willie Boy is Here* was delayed by the studio until late in 1969, when Redford had been proclaimed by the press an overnight sensation, after the success of *Butch Cassidy and the Sundance Kid*.

Polonsky wanted somebody young who looked good, not an older star like Kirk Douglas, and he knew that Redford was "an excellent actor, working in New York in television and in plays. He was very obliging, very obedient, but he didn't seem to have any particular knowledge of the West then, although he now has an interest for these things."[3] Redford had already made quite a few films, including *Barefoot in the Park* (1967) with Jane Fonda, directed by Gene Sacks from the Neil Simon play that he had performed on Broadway in 1963 with Elizabeth Ashley, and he was based in New York. However, he was born and raised in the West, in the Santa Monica and Van Nuys neighborhoods of Los Angeles, and was an avid outdoorsman with a home in Utah; so he was a good choice to play a cowboy on horseback with a knowledge of the desert wilderness. Polonsky said: "Redford is a good climber, a mountain man; he wanted to do his own climbing. He saved my life even, because I was taking a shot on top of a mountain and I backed right off the mountain. Redford was on a ledge ten feet below and caught me."[4] Redford showed in this film the same desire to do his own stunts that he would display in *Butch Cassidy and the Sundance Kid*, because he felt a personal identification with this kind of Westerner, as he would with athletes such as the skier in *Downhill Racer* (1969) and the baseball player in *The Natural* (1984).

Polonsky recognized Redford's input as an actor, because he knew about the importance of actors in a film and he would teach his USC university students that actors are the ones who bring the script to life. He said that Redford "made an enormous contribution. He's very good as an actor playing parts where he fundamentally is defeated in everything he wants."[5] Redford has been particularly adept at portraying this kind of flawed hero, probably because from a young age he was able to see the hypocrisy of American society.

Redford had his own reasons for accepting the role: "I liked the script. I liked what it was trying to say. I was attracted to the idea of playing a simple man who grows. He's a loner who can't make the adjustment to modern society. He was raised with Indians. He has no respect for the white community's attitude of 'I think I'll go out and kill me a few Indians,' but he has to maintain law and order. In the process of the chase he discovers a lot about himself. In the beginning he's an uncommitted man; at the end he's committed. He learns, he grows."[6]

Sheriff Cooper is a man who lives under the shadow of his father's legend, "that great western murdering Marshal" as Elizabeth calls him, a traditional lawman of the West who ironically was killed in a saloon by a drunken Indian, a horse thief. Some of his father's old cronies, like Ray Calvert (Barry Sullivan), whom Willie Boy calls "old bastard Calvert, that Indian killer," are in the posse that is chasing after Willie Boy and recount with nostalgia their exploits killing Indians. Coop shuts them up with a curt remark, "We better forget about the good old days right now."

Coop knows and respects Willie. When the cowboy that the Indian had hit with the cue-stick in the pool-hall complains, "He tried to kill me," he observes, "If he tried to kill you, you'd be dead." He's also influenced by Liz's caring attitude towards the Indians; it's because Liz wants the young Indian woman to return home that Coop decides to go after Willie Boy, after he kills Lola's father and runs off with her, and he pursues him even though he thinks that an Indian killing another Indian should be of no interest to the Sheriff's department. Coop then leaves the chase to meet his superior, Sheriff Frank Wilson, in Riverside, where a visit from President William Taft is expected. He goes back, after confused reports about Willie having wounded Calvert—while shooting at the horses to slow down the posse—are twisted into wildly exaggerated newspaper stories about an Indian uprising to overthrow the US government and a plot to assassinate the President. He tells Liz, "I should have stayed with that posse. I didn't do my job, the one time in my life I had a job to do. You and your goddamn Indians, your goddamn talk. I know where he's going now and I'm going to get him, he belongs to me."

So this becomes a one-on-one chase between the now determined lawman and the fugitive Indian, while the rest of the posse trails behind. It's Coop who discovers Lola's dead body at Twentynine Palms, the Paiute Indian village (although the film doesn't say whether she killed herself to help Willie escape, or he killed her to prevent his woman from falling in the hands of their enemies).

Finally Coop faces Willie in an old-fashioned western-style shoot-out, playing hide-and-seek over a hill of boulders, until he finds the Indian and gives him a chance to turn around and defend himself, rather than killing him from the back. It is only after shooting him dead that the sheriff discovers that his opponent didn't have any more bullets in his rifle, a Winchester 30-30; and, while carrying his dead body over his shoulder down the hill, he reflects on the Indian's courage and sense of honor. Coop allows the body to be ceremonially burnt by the Indian policemen, and when Sheriff Wilson complains that he has nothing left to show, he declares bitterly: "Tell them we're all out of souvenirs."

As John Cawelti defines it, "The cowboy hero in his isolated combat with Indian or outlaw seemed to reaffirm the traditional image of masculine strength, honor and moral violence."[7] But, in this reversal of the traditional hero image, the sheriff realizes that his victory is hollow, and has not served the purpose of defending civilization. Lenihan comments, "The manhunt provides Deputy Coop (Robert Redford) a long-awaited challenge to prove his worth as a lawman after the routinized grind of riding guard on a reservation. For Coop, Willie Boy is a personal challenge rather than an enemy to society whom he must defeat for reasons of civil responsibility. Coop shares much of Willie Boy's contempt for society's false sense of respectability; and, only too late, he realizes the folly of the pursuit and that in killing Willie he has killed a part of himself."[8]

Redford would use a similar kind of ending in two films that he produced in those years, *Downhill Racer* (1969) and *The Candidate* (1972). He defines it a Pyrrhic victory, when the champion skier realizes he won by default, and the political candidate has won the election but no longer has convictions to implement. Therefore we can assume that Redford was in agreement with the philosophical conclusion of a leftist movie like *Tell Them Willie Boy is Here,* which was conceived as a criticism of a repressive society, and that he respected and admired Polonsky, a blacklisted writer-director—although he wasn't allowed to modify the ending of the film. (Polonsky tells an amusing story about Redford insisting that Coop should walk away at the end of the burial scene and leave the woman alone. So the director left the camera rolling as the actor walked off, kept shooting for a long time without saying "cut," then told Redford that he could have the film, if he wanted it, but it was not going to be in the picture).

The film *Tell Them Willie Boy is Here* was based on the 1960 non-fiction novel *Willie Boy, A Desert Manhunt* written by a 32-year-old journalist, Harry Lawton, who later became a professor at U.C. Riverside. Lawton saw this true story, which took place in 1909, two decades after the closing of the Frontier, as the "last great manhunt in the western tradition." He has a special indulgence for the posse lawmen, who, having closely known Wyatt Earp and his brothers, could be easily forgiven for bragging to newspapermen; it was their last chance for western glory, after thinking that the old violent West was dead. He also shows respect and understanding for the Paiute Indian, Willie Boy, and "his sheer feat of endurance," since he covered more than five hundred miles of desert wilderness on foot.

What is particularly interesting in Lawton's book is the exploration of how facts often became legends in the West, as they were reported in contemporary newspaper accounts, usually totally made up for effect and replete with literary flourishes. In the case of Willie Boy this happened at first because the death of the young Indian girl, Lolita, in order to raise the sympathies of female readers, was likened by local newspapers to the fate of literary heroine Ramona, the aristocratic Spanish girl who married an Indian chief and was shunned by society with tragic consequences. (The 1884 novel *Ramona* by Helen Hunt Jackson was turned into a film starring Loretta Young and Don Ameche directed by Henry King in 1936). A few days later bored newspapermen from the East who had arrived to dusty Riverside with President William Taft heard tales of the manhunt and embellished on it, making it their lead story. There was some concern over attempts on the president's life, since President William McKinley had been shot by a lone assassin a few years earlier (on September 1, 1901). And even though it turned out that Willie Boy was already dead—by his own hand, over a hundred miles away—several Indians sightings were combined as proof that over fifty warriors were coming from Nevada and Arizona to join their leader in a premeditated uprising to overthrow the American government.

We see in *Tell Them Willie Boy is Here* the concept of the Indian as outlaw hunted by a posse—like the roguish heroes of *Butch Cassidy and the Sundance Kid*—how paranoid government forces will hunt down a lone individual because they are scared of the freedom that he represents. In another counter-culture Western of the early 1970s, *Little Big Man* (1970) directed by Arthur Penn, Dustin Hoffman plays a white man raised by Indians who represent a culture that lives in harmony with nature, as opposed to the white men who "don't seem to know where the center of the earth is." This happened, says Cawelti, because of a "new fascination among the young with traditional Indian culture."[9] Indians and outlaws are on the same side because they represent the traditional way of life of simpler societies doomed to extinction versus the organized modern industrial world. These "counterculture Westerns," says Slotkin, promoted a "new Cult of the Indian," they "suggested that Native American culture might be a morally superior alternative to civilization."[10]

Starting with John Ford's *Cheyenne Autumn* (1964) these films coincided with an historical reevaluation of Native American history. "Leslie Fielder's *Return of the Vanishing American* (1966) forcibly reminded academic and public intellectuals of the Indians' significance as both fact and symbol in American history and culture and identified them as embodiments of a set of *alternative* values in sexuality, culture and politics."[11] Richard Slotkin connects this change in political consciousness to the organization of the American Indian Movement (AIM) in 1968. Redford was obviously a sympathizer of the movement, if not at this time then later on, when Peter Matthiessen's 1983 book In *the Spirit of Crazy Horse* would intensify his interest in AIM leader Leonard Peltier. We'll also notice how Redford in his book *The Outlaw Trail* (1978) speaks with admiration of Chief Joseph of the Nez Percé, "who made futile stands against the white man's Manifest Destiny," and laments the loss of dignity and spirit the Indians "suffered when they were forced to surrender their traditional way of life."[12]

As Lenihan notices, the Indian hero of *Tell Them Willie Boy Is Here*, like Paul Newman in *Hombre*, is "self assured" in his "contempt for the white man. When forced to kill an assailant out of self-defense," the hero becomes "the target of a ruthless manhunt."[13] There is a new political consciousness at work in this Left-cycle Western of the late 1960s, because the questioning and self-examination of the national character that had started in the post-war period "assumed even greater proportions, with the Vietnam war, ghetto and campus unrest, and the emergence of a New Left and counterculture to challenge traditional beliefs and institutions."[14] Polonsky's *Tell Them Willie Boy is Here* gives equal weight to the Indian couple's side of the story and presents the Indian outlaw's humanity as equal to that of the white man who is chasing him. This is a left-wing concept that counters a long tradition in American politics that views the enemy as a racial other, as Richard Slotkin explains in *Gunfighter Nation* (1992). From the time when the Puritans believed Indians could not be converted because they didn't have souls, this rhetoric of the frontier has served to justify American aggression: towards the Japanese during World War II, the Vietnamese during the Vietnam War, and Saddam Hussein, who was depicted by George Bush as an inhuman savage during the Gulf War of 1991 (the same thing would happen again in 2003 when Bush's son attacked Iraq).

Even though Polonsky's and Lawton's portrayal of the Indian was sympathetic, as in many alternative Westerns of this period, in recent years some historians have contested the facts presented in the film and in the book from a modern Indian perspective. In their 1994 book *The Hunt for Willie Boy, Indian Hating and Popular Culture*, James Sandos and Larry Burgess state that their reconstruction of the Willie Boy incident is the first done by professional historians, and that, with the help of the Chemehuevi families involved, they attempt to incorporate the Indian version of the story and reconcile it with the white perspective previously employed. They claim that it wasn't the newspaper accounts that created the western legend of "the last desert manhunt," but Harry Lawton's novelization and Abraham Polonsky's film. "An episode of local history in California was mythologized and raised to national significance because Robert Redford starred in a movie about it."[15] The cover of their book has a photo of Willie Boy and a larger one of Redford as Sheriff Coop. Lawson (who died in 2005 at 77) filed a libel suit and the court ordered that further editions of the book should include corrections.

Without going into their specific arguments, suffice it to say that a film like *Tell Them Willie Boy is Here* portrays Indians as human beings deserving of the same respect as any other race or culture, but it's still presenting the point of view of a white director who's using the Indian as a metaphor for his own political statement.

Abraham Polonsky was introduced by Harry Lawton to the Cahuilla Indians of the Morongo Reservation who endorsed his version of the story and participated in the filming as extras (their Malki Museum Press reprinted Lawton's book in 1976), and he is proud of the fact that in his film the Indians are real Indians, even though he couldn't a find a suitable girl to play Lola, so he chose Katherine Ross (who would play Redford's gilrfriend in *Butch Cassidy and the Sundance Kid*) and cast Robert Blake as Willie, upon Redford's suggestion (he had acted with Blake on *This Property is Condemned*, 1966, directed by Sydney Pollack). Polonsky even recorded the local tribal songs to preserve them, although, when the Smithsonian was looking for them years later, he found out that they had unfortunately been thrown away by a clerk clearing the shelves at Universal. So his respect for Indians and their cultural heritage is not in question, but Polonsky scoffs at Sandos and Burgess' search for authenticity about the true facts of the story: "I just used the historical background, but, as a storyteller, I put in anything I felt like. I invented all that stuff, it has nothing to do with history. *Willie Boy*, as far as I'm concerned, is not about the West, it's a very personal picture about something entirely different."[16]

This was the first chance that Abe Polonsky had to direct under his own name, since he had been blacklisted twenty years earlier, after directing the classic *Force of Evil* in 1948. He was determined to "make a picture about what happened to me during the blacklist, and I changed everything to fit the story I wanted to tell. Willie became a representative of what happened to people in the blacklist who came back and fought, even though it was a losing fight."[17] Polonsky was one of those people, having returned from France to testify when subpoenaed by the House Un-American Activities Committee, regardless of the danger. "I was stubborn. I didn't think it was right for them to chase me out of my own country, so I went back and let them serve me; and they took my passport away, so I couldn't go abroad. That was very romantic, but I felt it was worthwhile fighting a losing battle to keep the spirit alive."[18]

Polonsky's main point was to show that "Indians are people, as we are people."[19] He showed how the two heroes, the Indian and the sheriff, were symbolically brothers in the scene where Coop bends over to drink at a stream, and, seeing Willie's handprint in the mud, puts his own hand inside it. His film is "a psychological story, fundamentally, about the relation between two men who know and respect each other."[20] This attitude was similar to the respect for the Indian way of life in the mountain wilderness that Robert Redford would show in *Jeremiah Johnson* (1972), a film that he produced.

Tell Them Willie Boy is Here, because of its sympathetic view of the Indians and the liberal politics of its authors, Polonsky and Lawton, is often mentioned by critics in the same context as other films of the late 1960s early 1970s that have a pro-Indian point of view, such as *Little Big Man* (1970) and *A Man Called Horse* (1970). Also, like *High Noon* (1952) with Gary Cooper, directed by Fred Zinnemann and written by blacklisted writer Carl Foreman, it offers a metaphor for the behavior of many American citizens during the Communist scare of the McCarthy era, and makes a critical statement about American society. Redford was in agreement with what the script was trying to say, as he would prove with his later films that were critical of right-wing politics, such as *The Candidate* (1972) and *All The President's Men* (1976).

2. BUTCH CASSIDY AND THE SUNDANCE KID

Outlaws as Western heroes

Butch Cassidy and the Sundance Kid (1969) is a pivotal film in Robert Redford's career because it made him a star and gave him the clout in the industry that he longed for, to gain more control over future projects, after working for years in movies that he didn't particularly like and getting in trouble with studios for refusing to do films when he was under contract. This film also established his persona as a western outlaw, an image that Redford has consistently been identified with and that he himself embraces, having often expressed his sympathy for Indians and outlaws.

The script by William Goldman was originally called *The Sundance Kid and Butch Cassidy*, but when Paul Newman was picked for the role of Cassidy, the names were reversed. Newman was a star at the height of his popularity, who had already played memorable western heroes in *Hombre* (1966), *Hud* (1963) and *The Left-Handed Gun* (1962). One of the problems the filmmakers were facing was that Redford was not a well-known actor at the time; in fact producer Richard Zanuck wanted to cast Steve McQueen (Jack Lemmon, Warren Beatty and Marlon Brando were also considered). But George Roy Hill and Paul Newman (upon a recommendation from Joanne Woodward) insisted on the more youthful actor, who fit the part because similarly not much is known about Harry Alonzo Longabaugh, the dangerous outlaw nicknamed the Sundance Kid from a place in Wyoming. Robert Leroy Parker, who was known as Butch Cassidy, the leader of the

"Hole in the Wall" gang, had picked Longabaugh as his partner, after his longtime associate William Ellsworth "Elzy" Lay ended up in jail in 1899; in fact, Butch's sister, Lula Betenson, who visited the set and met the actors playing the real-life outlaws, claims in her book that "most of the episodes in the movie involved Elzy Lay instead of the Sundance Kid."[1]

Goldman says that he needed to establish Sundance's character in that first scene where he's playing cards (black-jack); the director says that he framed Redford's face in a tight close-up, during the opening sequence in sepia-toned black and white, because "I wanted to use the first scene as an introduction to Redford, give him a little weight, a stature as a player."[2] Warshow had defined the Westerner as "a man of leisure" whom we usually encounter "standing at the bar, or playing poker—a game which expresses perfectly his talent for remaining relaxed in the midst of tension."[3] In this situation, when Butch eventually utters the name Sundance, the other player realizes his mistake in accusing the legendary outlaw of cheating, and the audience learns that the Sundance Kid had a reputation as the fastest gun in the West. The Westerner "can ride a horse faultlessly, keep his countenance in the face of death, and draw his gun a little faster and shoot a little straighter than anyone he's likely to meet."[4] At this point the audience is treated to a spectacular demonstration of Sundance's shooting prowess, "and we know one thing," says Goldman, "you don't much want to mess with him. The man is a bomb, capable of exploding at any time."[5]

As Redford describes Sundance, "There was a reason why he was the fastest gun in the West at that time, because he used his gun a lot. He's aloof, he's a loner, somewhat sullen, and to the outsider he's a very distant kind of guy; maybe even a bit schizoid."[6] The director found some similarities between the character and Redford's personality. "I wanted Bob in the picture from the beginning. He is a tremendous acting talent; he's also a very independent, hard-nosed man, who goes pretty much his own way. Those were qualities that worked very well for Sundance, including genuine warmth under a cool exterior. Sundance was Butch's opposite in almost every way. He was a deadly killer, a man of sudden violences and titanic drunks. He had no friends, really, except Butch, and the extraordinary thing was the closeness of their friendship and the fact that it lasted all their lives."[7] On this set Robert Redford and Paul Newman would form an enduring friendship that lasts to this day, as witnessed by Redford's 2005 interview with Newman for his Sundance series *Iconoclasts*.

It was Sundance's warm friendship with Cassidy that attracted Redford to the role, and also what made the film a success with the public. "I was surprised by the kind of success it had, I wasn't prepared for that. As to why, I think it had to do with more than guys running out of time, it had to do with a certain kind of bonding and connection, a real friendship—whether it's between male and female, or female/female, or male/male, it doesn't matter—when you can put that on a film in a very real, warm and entertaining way, it has a lot of currency. It was probably one of the first of the buddy films. As I remember, Goldman was very influenced by *Gunga Din,* about male bonding, male friendships."[8] As Molly Haskell notes, "The theme of male camaraderie has cropped up with increasing self-consciousness and sentimentality in recent years: in the reflective old-gunfighter Westerns of the sixties and seventies," among which she quotes Sam Peckinpah's *Ride the High Country* (1962), "and in the young-gunfighter ones."[9] *Butch Cassidy and the Sundance Kid* fits in this category because the close friendship between the two men is the supporting structure of the film.

The banter between the two friends, who don't hesitate to insult each other in a humorous way, is the thread that sustains this story of two outlaws whose world has changed because of the advances of technology. When banks adopt new security systems and train robbers are chased by an invincible posse, the only way for our heroes to maintain their lifestyle is to go to South America, a place that in the early 1900s, Butch says, was like California during the Gold Rush of the 1850's. What Goldman found most moving about these two heroes is that they escaped; they're not traditional western heroes like John Wayne or Gary Cooper, who would feel an obligation to stay and fight, "because that's what brave men did."[10] Although Goldman rejects the political interpretation of the film that likened the super-posse to the government in the Vietnam War era—to Lyndon Johnson and Richard Nixon trying to catch draft dodgers escaping abroad to avoid being sent to war—it is the obvious sympathy of the filmmakers for the freedom of the outlaws that made *Butch Cassidy and the Sundance Kid* such an appealing movie and firmly implanted it into popular culture.

Butch Cassidy, in the film's interpretation, is a lovable outlaw who never killed anyone, and preferred to use his brain and his sense of humor to get his way. He boasts, "I got vision and the rest of the world wears bifocals," and Sundance kids him, "You just keep thinking Butch; that's what you're good at." Butch knows that he's over the hill, "Every day you get older. That's a law." But until the end, when they're seriously wounded in San Vicente, Bolivia and under attack from a whole battalion of soldiers, they exchange jokes that keep their hopes alive; Butch quips that he's considering going to Australia, where people speak English and where Sundance can finally learn to swim. George Roy Hill says of Butch Cassidy: "He led and controlled the most vicious gang in the West and still remained the most affable and good-natured outlaw in frontier history; everybody liked him, even the Pinkerton men."[11]

The filmmakers' nostalgia for the romantic days of the old West and their awareness of the outlaws' lore as a legend in the making is evident in the stylized touches that remind viewers of old silent films like *The Great Train Robbery* (in the opening credits sequence) and period photographs (in the New York montage), to conclude with the final freeze frame (where the background scene was shot with an 8x10 still camera) when our heroes are running to their death—but, in keeping with the comedic tone of the film, they are not killed in a gruesome bloodbath, as would have been the darker Sam Peckinpah style. Made in the same year, 1969, Peckinpah's *The Wild Bunch* (another name for Butch Cassidy's gang) treated a similar theme of aging outlaw heroes out of step with the times who are also pursued by a hired posse and take refuge in a Latin country, Mexico. Robert Ray notices: "Like *The Wild Bunch*, *Butch Cassidy and the Sundance Kid* attempted to buy time by transferring operations to a more primitive country (Bolivia) where, presumably, conditions would still permit lifestyles that had become impossible in the United States. But the promise of Latin America as a frontier proved illusory."[12]

The affection for the unencumbered outlaw lifestyle, the love for the outdoors and the appreciation for the beauty of the western landscape of open vistas, mountains and valleys, permeates the memories of the filmmakers shooting *Butch Cassidy and the Sundance Kid*. Paul Newman recalls that the camaraderie was contagious and they had a terrific time: "I'm nostalgic for those days when people made films; that's maybe one of the reasons why it works. I suspect it has something to do with the delight of the filmmakers while they were making it."[13] Redford confesses:

"It had the best locations imaginable, at least in my mind. Zion National Park, Durango Colorado, incredible scenery, topography, varied, western, we rode through that, it was a joy; then Mexico. It was pretty blessed in terms of the environment that we were working in, I had a great time."[14] The most delighted of all was Robert Crawford, the young writer-director of the documentary *The Making of Butch Cassidy and the Sundance Kid*: "I couldn't get over that somebody was paying me to be out there in that country, enjoying that beauty and nature and freedom. It was one of the great thrills of all time to participate in making a film."[15]

These confessions prove that the male stars and filmmakers shooting the picture enjoyed the opportunity to play cowboys and identified with the western heroes they were portraying. Redford was so proud of his physical prowess that he insisted in doing all his own stunts, like jumping on the moving train. He claimed he was pretty good at any sport, like skiing or tennis, and challenged George Roy Hill to the contest of his choice; the director, who had been laid up by a bad back, picked fencing, because he knew that Crawford had been a fencing champion, and tricked Redford into accepting the young filmmaker as his stand-in. Redford, who lost the duel but defended himself honorably, commented: "I like to play practical jokes on people, but that was brilliant; because I suddenly realized I'd been completely had. You just had to appreciate it."[16]

The flip side of all this male bonding and tough-guy derring-do was that women were not included in the fun—in the film, as in real life—on a Hollywood movie set of the late 1960's. Crawford says that, even though he was a newly-wed, his wife was not welcome on the set, since even the key people didn't bring their wives in that period; "It breeds camaraderie, but it's hard on family life."[17] The female protagonist of the film, Katherine Ross, who played Etta Place, the third side of the love triangle between Butch and Sundance, was banned from the set, before she even started filming, because of an unforgivable transgression into the male-dominated world of behind-the-camera professionals.

This anecdote from the shooting illustrates the attitude of male western heroes towards their women and shows that, even in a counter-culture Western like *Butch Cassidy and the Sundance Kid*, the new message of feminism had not yet reached the Hollywood film community. Later

Redford would become more aware of the importance of women in the films that he produced and directed, from *The Milagro Beanfield War* (1986) to *The Legend of Bagger Vance* (2000), but probably at this time the male-chauvinism of this set didn't bother him, even though he remembers a strange comment from Joanne Woodward: "When we were making it, Paul's wife told me, you and Paul have better chemistry than me and Paul."[18]

Katherine Ross was in a relationship with cinematographer Conrad Hall (she had met him on the set of *Tell Them Willie Boy is Here*) and felt confident enough to operate one of five cameras, an Arriflex, when they needed an extra operator during the shooting of a distant scene of stuntmen riding horses on a ridge. Hall had given her permission and was pulling focus for her, while the director was sitting nearby without voicing any objections. It was only after the shooting day was over that Ross realized how furious Hill really was; she had incurred the director's wrath and was not allowed to be on the set from that moment on, unless she was in a scene. This is how Ross recalls the incident: "I had this fantasy of becoming the first woman in the camera union, because there weren't any women at that moment in time; and I practiced doing this shot, just panning these guys along the railroad tracks. I feel very naive and it was not very bright on my part; but evidently this was very upsetting to several people; one of them was the director, who chose not to say anything until after the fact. It was very devastating to me; in a way that incident, or that action, haunted me for the rest of the film."[19]

Hill had nothing but praise for Katherine Ross' feminine beauty: "She came on the picture basically because I thought she was the sexiest girl I'd ever seen; she was ravishingly beautiful and I was pretty much blind to any other possible talent."[20] But it was a different story when a woman showed any technical expertise behind the camera, or wanted to get involved in the comedic bantering between the two guys. "I got to be the straight man," says Ross, "that really was Etta's part in that. It was frustrating for me; when everybody's laughing, you want people to laugh at you too."[21]

Goldman's concept of Etta (Ethel) Place is that she was a schoolteacher, not a prostitute, as others thought, "Because it was such a tough life out there, I just don't think anybody that stunningly pretty could have lived as a whore."[22] Hill says that Etta probably had a sexual relationship with both

Butch and Sundance, but he couldn't show that in this kind of mainstream film, so he only suggested it at the end of the famous bicycle scene, which was underscored by the Burt Bacarach's song "Raindrops Falling on My Head."

Goldman hated the traditional role of women in western films; he particularly despised Grace Kelly's attitude in *High Noon*, of holding Gary Cooper back from fighting for fear that he would get killed, and he wanted to do something different. "What I did with Etta, very consciously, is that, in every scene that she's in, she gives a surprise."[23] In the introductory scene we're to believe that she's about to be raped at gunpoint by Sundance, when he asks her to undress and let her hair down, then we discover that she's his girlfriend; the next morning she cavorts on the bicycle with Butch, and we realize there's a sexual attraction between them as well; later she teaches the guys Spanish, so they can rob banks in South America, and she's talking to Butch on the other side of the wall, while she's in bed with Sundance; finally she leaves South America because she doesn't want to see them die, as she had announced earlier, in an emblematic statement of female submissiveness. "I'm twenty-six and I'm single, and I teach school and that's the bottom of the pit. And the only excitement I've ever known is sitting in the room with me now. So I'll go with you and I won't whine, and I'll sew your socks and stitch you when you're wounded, and anything you ask of me I'll do, except one thing: I won't watch you die. I'll miss that scene if you don't mind."

Molly Haskell quotes this self-effacing comment to point out that "the schoolteacher is generally seen—and generally sees herself—as a pitiable figure, synonymous with 'old maid.' They all flee at the first opportunity, and with the first man that gives them a nod, an occupation that by society's lights is a fate worse than death."[24] Yet that of schoolmarm is the only acceptable profession for so many western heroines—from *The Virginian* (1929) to *High Noon* (1954)—who represent Eastern civilization for the western heroes; these "good women" are contrasted by the dark females, prostitutes and dance-hall girls, "who are a feminine embodiment of the hero's savage, spontaneous side."[25] This dichotomy had its first literary representation in the figures of blond Alice and dark-haired Cora from James Fenimore Cooper's *The Last of the Mohicans* (1850) and had been repeated in countless Westerns. In a recent version of *The Last of the Mohicans* (1992) director Michael Mann operated a reversal; Alice and not Cora has dark hair and she has a love affair with the dark-haired Hawkeye, a man raised by Indians, rather than with the blond Englishman Hayward. In *Butch Cassidy and the Sundance Kid* the heroine is dark-haired and possesses a clear sensuality; so the intentions of the filmmakers might have been to give Etta a pro-active role as an equal partner with the guys, but, in fact, her position was unequivocally subordinate to the love between the men.

From a modern critical perspective, such as that of Eve Sedgwick Kosofsky, which explores the gay and lesbian subtexts in literature and films, you could say that Etta, the female corner of the love triangle, serves as the mirror into which the homosexual love between the two men is reflected. Kosofsky says that her 1985 book *Between Men* "focused on the oppressive effects on women and men of a cultural system in which male-male desire became widely intelligible primarily by being routed through triangular relations involving a woman."[26] Joan Mellen in her 1977 book *Big Bad Wolves* also contended that *Butch Cassidy and the Sundance Kid* was indeed a thinly disguised homosexual love story.

Molly Haskell wrote in the early 1970s, "Sexual desire is not the point, nor 'homoeroticism' the term for these relationships," rather it's a kind of "love in which men understand and support each other, speak the same language, and risk their lives to gain each other's respect. But this is also a delusion; the difficulties of the adventure disguise the fact that this is the easiest of loves: a love that is adolescent, presexual, tacit, the love of one's semblance, one's mirror reflection."[27] With the optimism typical of the early feminist movement, Haskell was hopeful that men would change: "Men have been deprived of the physical grounds for the testing of their virility and those magical mirrors women held up to their egos. It is, still, a painful transitional period. And they haven't yet adjusted to a new definition of masculinity, one that would include courage and bravery in personal relationships."[28]

Redford has shown in his later work and his personal life—by being married to the same woman for thirty years, fathering and rearing three children as an involved parent—that he has not remained stuck in this kind of adolescent love between men; but he couldn't help being attracted to the boyish adventures of charming outlaws in a film that belonged to the counter-culture but was inherently escapist. He writes in his foreword to Lula Parker's book that these "badmen" were, in fact, "kids who never grew up or high spirited men whose sense of fun and pranks couldn't be contained by the law." In his view Butch and Sundance "captured a piece of our past that was nostalgic. To us it was also synonymous with romance, free spirit, and the pure frontier sense of enterprise."[29]

Butch Cassidy and The Sundance Kid was a success with the public precisely because of its light tone and the likability of its stars, Newman and Redford. The film hit a chord in the popular consciousness because, in a time of cultural revolution like the late 1960's early 1970's, Butch and Sundance could be seen as romantic symbols of individual freedom and youthful rebellion engaged in a doomed fight against the system. Michael Coyne comments, "The film's light-hearted iconoclasm and good-humored cynicism caught the mood of late 1960s America. In a time of ever-growing disaffection over the pervasive influence of corporate power structures and the seemingly interminable involvement in Vietnam, *Butch* romanticized its renunciation of modern America with cool, laid-back irreverence rather than with blood-soaked fervor . . . Yet, if *Butch*'s style initially seems overly frivolous, it is also covertly critical of America's political and corporate Establishment. As non-conformists, dropouts and casualties of military violence, Butch and Sundance were clearly ideal icons for America's counterculture in the late 1960s."[30]

Through the years Butch Cassidy has been often portrayed as a Robin Hood of the West, who stole from the rich to give to the poor. Like many other "actual western badmen like Billy the Kid, Jesse James and Wild Bill Hickock," says Cawelti, "the outlaw was presented as a decent person who had been unjustly treated by the rich and powerful."[31] He had become a folk hero for the oppressed, by taking the side of the small homesteaders against the cattle barons, the banks and the railroad magnates. "Two of the most successful Westerns of 1969, *The Wild Bunch* and *Butch Cassidy and the Sundance Kid*, actually went so far as to reverse the usual pattern of the formula Western and to present the unregenerate, lawless outlaw as a sympathetic figure by expressing a definite sense of regret at his elimination by the agents of law and order. They are professional criminals rather than men driven to a life of crime by some wrong done to them. Yet, since they represent a more spontaneous, individualistic and free way of life, their destruction by the brutal, massive and corrupt agencies of the state is presented critically."[32]

Robert Ray says: "Since *Red River* (1948), the Western as a form had been preoccupied with the dying out of radically individualistic lifestyles. This preoccupation intensified in the sixties (*The Man Who Shot Liberty Valance, Ride the High Country, Hud, Hombre*) until by the end of the decade it had become almost the genre's *only* theme." He points out that almost all the Left movies, specifically *Butch Cassidy and the Sundance Kid* and *The Wild Bunch*, "used outlaws or outsiders to represent the counterculture's own image of itself as in flight from a repressive society," which was embodied by the "nameless, faceless Pinkerton men relentlessly pursuing Butch Cassidy and the Sundance Kid." But he concludes that this "new" American cinema was "superficially radical, internally conservative," because, while acknowledging the anachronism of outdated lifestyles that were doomed to extinction, these Left-cycle Westerns "regarded sympathetically its heroes' violence, portraying it as the last possible expression of individual freedom." Their romanticized endings apotheosized "heroes who clearly embodied the traditional mythology." Ray uses the freeze frame at the end of *Butch Cassidy and the Sundance Kid* as an example of a New Wave device that does not imply the revolutionary intentions of a filmmaker like Godard. "In aestheticizing its heroes' deaths, the Left cycle perpetuated the values that it had nominally discredited: individualism, self-sufficiency, and escapism. In doing so, it further blurred the distinctions between itself and the Right."[33]

To bring the discussion back to Redford's political convictions, I will point out that he did not actively participate in the radical movements of the late 1960s; he did not demonstrate against the Vietnam War for example, although he was opposed to war in general. In the 1960s he was struggling to find work as an actor to support his family; his youthful rebellion had happened a decade earlier, when he had left college to go to Europe and study painting, in the bohemian vein of that time.

In any case, even if it didn't subvert the conventional Hollywood formulas or advance the revolutionary cause, the success of *Butch Cassidy and the Sundance Kid* generated a new interest in historical studies about these real-life outlaws. It inspired the book by Larry Pointer, *In Search of Butch*

Cassidy, where it's established that Butch and Sundance didn't die in Bolivia, an autobiographical book by Cassidy's sister who tried to justify her brother's life of violence, *Butch Cassidy, My Brother,* for which Redford wrote the introduction, and a book by Robert Redford himself, *The Outlaw Trail.*

3. THE OUTLAW TRAIL

Legendary hideouts of the West

Robert Redford, who had become personally identified with the image of a western movie hero on the strength of *Butch Cassidy and the Sundance Kid*, was asked by *National Geographic* magazine in 1975 to take a trip retracing the steps of the famous western outlaws—from Canada to Mexico through Montana, Wyoming, Utah, Colorado and New Mexico—in the company of a small group of people and a photographer, Jonathan Blair. Redford fittingly started his journey at Hole in the Wall, Wyoming, the hideout of Butch Cassidy and Sundance's Wild Bunch gang, and ended it in Circleville, Utah, at the home of Lula Parker, Butch Cassidy's sister. The result of this adventure, conducted for the most part on horseback with only the camping equipment and provisions that the actual outlaws would have carried in their time, was published in 1978 in a book written by Redford himself, *The Outlaw Trail, a Journey Through Time*.

Redford writes in the foreword: "The Outlaw Trail. It was a name that fascinated me—a geographical anchor of western folklore. Whether real or imagined, it was a name that, for me, held a kind of magic, a freedom, a mystery." He would later say: "It isn't an affection for outlaws I have. It was more that I identified with them."[1] Redford's book begins with a quote from Vardis Fisher's novel *Mountain Man* (which had inspired his movie *Jeremiah Johnson*): "Why any man would willingly live in a city, with its infernal stinks and noises, he would never know, . . . when he could come

West to God's finest sculptures . . . and be his own lord and king and conscience, with no law except that of the brave . . ." In their common love for the unspoiled beauty of the western landscape and their individualistic lifestyle, a connection is made in *The Outlaw Trail* between all rugged western heroes, not only outlaws like Jesse James and Butch Cassidy, but lawmen like Wyatt Earp and Bat Masterson, even frontier women like Calamity Jane and Indians like Chief Joseph.

Redford defines the outlaw trail, between 1870 and 1910, as a "lawless area where any man with a past or a price on his head was free to roam 'nameless,' provided he was good with a gun, fast on a horse, cleverer than the next man, could run as fast as he could cheat, trusted no one, had eyes on the back of his head and a fool's sense of adventure."[2] He expresses on his admiration for the outlaw, as opposed to the lawman, "I had become increasingly intrigued by the many outlaws who had demonstrated wit and brains unmatched by any but the most brilliant in legitimate society."[3] He adds: "In truth, the line between the 'good guy' and the 'bad guy' in the West was often blurred, and many of the outlaws, in spite of their errant and often violent natures, were men of extraordinary skill and cunning, who by comparison made the lawmen look pathetic."[4]

Very often though, in the history of the West, the outlaws became lawmen and the lawmen outlaws, as Rita Parks explains: "A brief look at career highlights of Bat Masterson, Wyatt Earp, and Wild Bill Hickock offers a convincing proof that these were men to be reckoned with—gunmen and lawmen at the same time." When he was town marshal in Tombstone, "Earp's image was that of a dangerous man. Today is that of a courageous peace officer." James Butler "Wild Bill" Hickok, when he was brought to Abilene in 1871 and "hired as marshal to help control gambling dens and brothels, enforced the law principally through his established reputation as a gunfighter."[5]

This connection between outlaw hero and official hero—as two sides of the same western male ideal that have to come together in order to fight against a true evil, such as murdering cattlemen—is explored in many Westerns of the post-war period, as Robert Ray illustrates in *A Certain Tendency of the Hollywood Cinema*. For example in *My Darling Clementine* (1946), directed by John Ford, Wyatt Earp (Henry Fonda) needs the help of the gambling outlaw Doc Holliday (Victor Mature) to defeat the Clantons. In

The Man Who Shot Liberty Valance (1962), also directed by Ford, an aging gunfighter played by John Wayne, with his violent ways of dealing with the outlaws hired by the cattle barons, finds himself on the losing side of the battle to civilize the West, in comparison with the young lawyer played by James Stewart. In the end, Wayne is identified as the real hero, the man who shot Liberty Valance, but the newspapermen refuse to print Stewart's confession with the famous line, "When the legend becomes fact, print the legend."

In a contemporary Western such as *Wyatt Earp* (1994) directed by Lawrence Kasdan, Kevin Costner as Wyatt Earp turns from lawman into outlaw when the fight with the cattle barons becomes personal after his brother gets killed, and his old friend Doc Holliday (Dennis Quaid) does the same. Kasdan explains the moral implications of the old code of the West, as they apply to today's world situation: "The problem, which Wyatt Earp experiences throughout his life, is that, when you become brutal in the face of brutality, you must live with that for the rest of your life and there are consequences. When we look across the ocean at certain situations in the world, the natural American response is to go in there and 'clean up the town,' just as Wyatt Earp was always asked to do. But the fact is that some situations cannot be solved so simply, and America has found out—to its great expense and pain in the last thirty years—that we are not the Wyatt Earps of the world and we cannot solve all the problems. In fact, we can't even solve the problems in our own country."[6]

With Kasdan, just as with Redford, the sympathy for the outlaw comes from a leftist point of view. Robert Ray puts Redford's film *Butch Cassidy and the Sundance Kid* on the left side of a list of films from the late 1960's and early 1970's, with other Westerns like *The Wild Bunch* (1969) by Sam Peckinpah, *Little Big Man* (1970) by Arthur Penn, *McCabe and Mrs. Miller* (1971) by Robert Altman.

Redford certainly identifies with what Ray calls the post-war Western's preoccupation with "the dying out of individualistic lifestyles," which intensified in the 1960's and is exemplified in movies like *Hud* and *Hombre* directed by Martin Ritt and starring Paul Newman. The first words of *The Outlaw Trail* read: "The West today is in a state of change—and siege. Many Westerners are worried about the invasion of their land, space and water."[7] While he was making *The Electric Horseman* (1979), where the exploitation of the horse serves as a metaphor for the commercialization of the cowboy, Redford was aware of the disappearance of the unspoiled West and was determined to do what he could to preserve it. "It's hard to go anywhere where there isn't some sign of development or nature-rape. There's no frontier left . . . and that's why I'm so concerned with western politics. I suspect that it's all a horserace, between those that develop and those that preserve."[8] As a director he would examine the clash of Indian, Mexican and Anglo cultures in New Mexico in *The Milagro Beanfield War* (1988) based on the novel by John Nichols, and the value of individual resistance in a situation where the water rights of the people who have cultivated the land for centuries are taken away by greedy real-estate developers.

In his book Redford laments the disappearance of the cowboy as a fixture of western life, due to the decline in the ranching business, and he misses their colorful storytelling exploits around the campfire. "Will Rogers is the most recognizable prototype I can recall—spinning a yarn, twirling a rope, winking an eye, and never giving away whether the tale was truth or fiction."[9] He describes some of the typical aspects of the cowboy lifestyle, when he writes about the importance of the hat, "the Stetson is the cowboy's mantle, his security blanket,"[10] and of the necessity of knowing about horses, so as not to be dubbed a tenderfoot, "cowboying requires real knowledge of a horse and his capabilities."[11] He would explore this theme as a director twenty years later in *The Horse Whisperer* (1998), where he plays a rancher with a gift for healing horses. In the book Redford recounts with obvious longing an episode when he ran into a pack of wild horses led by a beautiful untamed stallion, "I couldn't deny the feeling of envy this sight provoked."[12] He probably remembered this emotion when he was shooting the ending of *The Electric Horseman*, where the wild stallions represent the freedom in nature that the former rodeo cowboy is looking for.

The writing of *The Outlaw Trail* served as a pause for Redford, a time to meditate about turning 40 and explore other interests besides movies. "I go through bursts of energy, I guess. I'll do two or three films, back to back, and then take off for a few years to do something else. That's been a constant pattern. But this time I just moved into a totally different area. I wrote a book, built a solar home, traveled, read a lot and thought about turning 40. I wanted to farm and I started that (he has been growing alfalfa, corn, barley and wheat on his land in Utah). And I wanted to study alternative energy technology, to really feel that I knew what I was talking about."[13] He would continue to pursue those interests throughout his life and use this knowledge to step up his fight against the country's dependence on oil in recent years.

4. JEREMIAH JOHNSON

A mountain man on the frontier

Jeremiah Johnson (1972) is a central film in Redford's filmography, because he produced it and shot it on his own mountain property in Utah, with the help of his director friend and fellow Westerner Sydney Pollack. Therefore Redford was able to express many of his own ideas about the West and his chosen lifestyle, between New York City and the unspoiled mountains of Utah, where he built a wood and stone house for his family with his own hands. He understands the myth of the Westerner as a man that, like Buffalo Bill Cody "stood between savagery and civilization,"[1] and is aware of the antinomies posited by Jim Kitses in *Horizons West*: wilderness stands for the individual, nature and the West, civilization for the community, culture and the East.

In *Jeremiah Johnson* Robert Redford plays a young soldier who, as the opening narration goes, "wanted to be a mountain man and said goodbye to whatever life was down there below. He was a man of proper wit and adventurous spirit, suited to the mountains." When he reaches a bustling trading post by the Green River in Colorado, populated by Indians on double-hulled canoes, he gets himself a Hawker rifle, a horse, a pack mule, traps and supplies; he wants to know where to find "bear, beaver and other critters worth cash money when skinned," and he's told "Ride due West to the sunset, turn left at the Rocky Mountains."

The myth of the mountain men—the nomadic fur trappers who roamed the Rockies in the mid 1800s—has long been part of the western legend. Henry Nash Smith calls them "the first generation of fictional Wild Western heroes after Cooper," and "symbols of anarchic freedom."[2] The successor of Natty Bumppo (the hero of James Fenimore Cooper's *Lethearstocking Tales*) and Daniel Boone (the Kentucky hunter and explorer that was adopted by Shawnee Indians), the mountain man was more uncivilized, he had adopted many more Indian ways than the typical pioneer. "His costume, his speech, his outlook on life, often enough his Indian squaw, gave him a decidedly savage aspect."[3]

Redford must have enjoyed the progressive transformation he underwent in *Jeremiah Johnson*, from clean-cut soldier to bearded savage dressed in animal furs; it was his chance to trash the blond golden boy image that he felt had been inflicted upon him since *Barefoot in the Park* and that would haunt him for years to come, preventing him from being considered a "serious actor." He says: "Cement begins to form around that image, and you have to work very hard to break through it; so you may not be able to do all the work you want to do, because of people locking you into some particular type. I don't hate the sex symbol image, I just find it restrictive sometimes, and it gets tiresome."[4]

Redford also relished exploring the life of the real mountain men who inspired the film; with Sydney Pollack, he helped exhume John Johnson's remains from the Veterans cemetery in Westwood and return them to the place where the former mountain man spent the last few years of his life as a sheriff: Cody, Wyoming, the town founded in 1896 by William F. "Buffalo Bill" Cody. In Cody's Old Trail Town there's a monument to the American Mountain Man, which commemorates Jim Bridger, the fur trapper and explorer who claimed to have discovered the Yellowstone geysers, and John Colter, a hunter for Lewis and Clark. Not coincidentally, in that same place, where Bob Edgar has collected famous western buildings, is preserved the log cabin of Butch Cassidy and the Sundance Kid from Hole in the Wall, Wyoming.

John Milius had based his screenplay for *Jeremiah Johnson* on the 1958 book *Crow Killer, The Saga of Liver-Eating Johnson* by western writer Robert Bunker, co-written by Raymond W. Thorp, the man who had collected an oral history of the exploits of John Johnson from the tales of his fellow mountain men, like White-Eye Anderson and "Del" Gue. Johnson was not as famous as Buffalo Bill or Kit Carson, the most written about mountain men, but he was a legend among his peers for his huge size and the strength of his hands and feet. After the Crows killed his Flathead Indian wife and unborn child in 1847, he exacted revenge on their tribe and became the most hunted man in the Rockies, as more than twenty Crow braves challenged him in single combat through the years and were killed. In the film Del Gue says to Johnson, "Lucky they were Crows. The Apache would send fifty at once." Pollack comments: "There's a bit of machismo in this, but, once he did what he did, those Indians began to respect him so much that they would send only one man at the time after him; it became quite mythological, but it was true."[5]

Milius confesses that he loves the Apache most of all, because of their fierceness, and that he would go join them right now, if they were still "riding around the mountains of Arizona."[6] He had written the script for producer Joe Wizan and offered it to Warner Bros, when he was at the studio writing what would later become *Apocalypse Now*. Originally the role of Jeremiah Johnson was to be played by Lee Marvin, then by Clint Eastwood; and Sam Peckinpah was hired to direct. If that had happened, says Milius, it would have been a different, more ferocious film. When Robert Redford became involved, he wanted Sydney Pollack to direct (Pollack had already made a film about mountain men, *The Scalphunters*, 1968, with Burt Lancaster), and together they made "a sweeter movie, more politically correct." From Milius' point of view it's wrong to "portray Indians as hippies," he believes that we should tell the truth about the Indians. When he wrote the script for *Geronimo: An American Legend* (1994) directed by Walter Hill, he depicted Geronimo as a ferocious man, more like a lion or a tiger, and not as a victim. This interpretation is in the tradition of John Ford's *The Searchers* (1956) starring John Wayne, where, as Prats says, "the Indian hater himself devoutly wishes to be Indian, for in his Indianness lies his capacity to destroy the savage enemy," or *Hondo* (1953), also with John Wayne, "an attestation of the Western's persistent need to identify the champion of civilization by exalting his capacity for savagery."[7]

It's interesting to notice the difference between a violent view of the West—as that of Sam Peckinpah, Clint Eastwood, John Milius and Walter

Hill—macho men who feel a admiration for the Indians because they were warriors, and for outlaws and gunfighters because they were not afraid of killing, as opposed to the more gentle outlook expressed by Redford and Pollack, in *Jeremiah Johnson* and *The Electric Horseman*. The heroes of these films search for a harmonious connection between the white man and a natural environment that includes Indians and peaceful animals like horses.

While working together on the *Jeremiah Johnson*'s storyline, Redford and Pollack felt uneasy about showing the brutal massacre of Johnson's family by Indians and they struggled to find a reason for the violence. The director says: "I was terribly concerned, in 1971, about doing a movie in which a band of Native Americans senselessly slaughter a woman, which was the original story in Milius' script, that was taken from the story of the authentic Crow Killer. So most of the struggle and work that we did on it was to try to find some way to implicate him in his own demise, to find a way that his own behavior destroys him. It took months but we came up with the fact that he turned his back on civilization and decided to go away, and now civilization comes to him and asks him to do them a favor, and he does, for the best reasons, the wrong thing."[8]

Johnson violates a Crow's sacred burial ground, while helping cavalrymen rescue settlers whose wagons had broken down in the snow; his loyalty to the ways of the white man makes him go against the spiritual beliefs of the Indians, who still respected the land as sacred. The conflict is clearly expressed in the interchange between Johnson and a racist Reverend—traveling with a more respectful Army Lieutenant—who says: "Those are Christian families, Johnson, women and children, starving. You mean to tell me that you intend to let those people die?" Johnson agrees to go with the soldiers to show them the way, but hesitates to cross the burial ground; "Crows don't even come here, this is big medicine, they guard this place with spirits," to which the priest comments, "You've been up here too long, Johnson, believing in this."

Redford, who considers *Jeremiah Johnson* his most personal film, says: "Jeremiah was a man trying to make his way through life and still remain uncluttered by sophistication. But he discovers there is no place he can escape outside influences and codes. The Christian ethic gets him, when the soldiers come to take them through the burial ground, and that breaks the Indians' code."[9] By going back to live off the land, killing deer and buffalo and fishing from streams, in the solitude of the snow-capped mountains, Johnson had learned to respect the Indian way of life in harmony with nature; while for the Christian missionary the natives were simply savages restricted by their pagan superstitions and tribal religions. John Milius, by the way, considers mountain men to be the true pagans, "even more free than the Indians, because they didn't have superstition; they were totally unshackled by civilization or other constraints, they represented one of the ultimate examples of freedom."[10]

Redford had a more romantic outlook on the mountain man than Milius—for example, he eliminated any reference to the liver-eating from his movie—and was more in tune with the idealized feelings of the 1965 novel by Vardis Fisher, which the film was also based on, *Mountain Man, A Novel of Male and Female in the Early American West.* Redford talks about a spiritual experience he had while shooting the film on his own land, in the Wasach Mountains of Utah, when the helicopter with the camera left him alone in the snow to go get more film: "There was something wonderful about that day. While they were gone it was quite an experience. I lay back in the snow and savored the soundlessness of every moment—nothing but an occasional echo over the tip of a glacier."[11]

Vardis Fisher was a Mormon born in Idaho in 1895 whose father was a typical frontiersman who hated civilization and raised his family in a primitive home in the mountains with an almost religious work ethic. His upbringing was therefore not dissimilar to that of Norman Maclean's, the author of the autobiographical novella *A Rivers Runs Through It* that Redford would later make into a movie. Redford's wife, Lola Von Wagenen, was a Mormon from Provo, Utah; and, as soon as he had some money, Redford, who had become a lover of the outdoors while in college in Colorado, bought virgin land in Utah. Pollack, who also has a home in Utah close to Redford's house, contacted Fisher's widow and bought the rights to several of his novels.

Fisher's last novel before his death in 1968, *Mountain Man* is an ode not only to the beauty of nature and the courage of Samson John Minard, a giant of a man based on John Johnson, but to the power of women as uncompromising earth mothers, and the need of men for gentle female love. Ample space is given in his novel to the story of Kate Bowden, based on Jane Morgan, the woman who saw her sons and daughter brutally killed by Blackfeet Indians, and went insane with grief after killing the murderers with an axe. Kate spends her nights reading the Bible to the ghosts of her children, and Samson often joins her with his harmonica in singing hymns to God. When the Crows show compassion by burying Kate's body after her death in a snowstorm, Sam decides to smoke the peace pipe with the old Chief and forget his revenge against his wife's killers.

In the film the "crazy woman" doesn't have a central role, but after seeing a grave for himself next to her grave—arranged by Crows as a monument to a great warrior—Johnson understands that he has earned the respect of the Indians for his bravery. Del Gue had told him: "Most Indian tribes' greatness is figured on how mighty his enemies be." When Johnson meets the Crow Chief "Prints His Shirt Red" at the end—the same Indian who years before had been amused by his attempt to catch fish in the river with his bare hands, then had asked for his name when Johnson honored him with the gift of an elk pelt—the two men exchange a friendly salute.

Sydney Pollack says: "The ending turned out to be something that came entirely from Bob. The gesture had grief in it, it had anger, it had respect, it had sadness."[12] Redford explains: "The gesture was an ad-lib response to the frustration of the pain and confusion the character was experiencing. It indicated a respect for the enemy—what Rommel and Patton might have done if they had met."[13] As in *Tell Them Willie Boy is Here*, Redford in *Jeremiah Johnson* is a white man who learns that the Indian is his equal, if not his moral superior; and this realization is reflected in the real concerns that Robert Redford has expressed for the American Indians.

Jeremiah Johnson, like Samson in the Vardis novel, is a loner who finds happiness with his Indian wife, Swan, the sister of Flathead Chief Two Tongues, a Christian French-speaking Indian who had given her to Johnson as a gift, in exchange for Blackfeet ponies. The film shows how the silent mountain man warms up to family life with a woman who can't speak English, and his adopted son Caleb—the boy that Crazy Woman has entrusted to his care—who also doesn't speak much. Pollack says: "Nobody can talk to anybody in the movie, there isn't much dialogue, it's almost a silent movie. I made the kid deaf on purpose. It was interesting to me that he couldn't talk to his wife because she was Indian, he couldn't talk to the boy because the boy didn't talk, the crazy woman didn't talk at all;

so this sense of having to go for long periods of time without the pleasure of discourse was also part of the film." This way they were able to create a different kind of love story, "the sense of growing together by looking in the same direction, rather than at each other, which is the sort of narcissism of today's romances. It wasn't this kind of self-aware romance that he had with this Indian woman; he grew to love her because they shared a mutual distant goal of survival, creating a home and raising a family."[14]

In this pre-verbal state of a pure and natural lifestyle the male hero finds fulfillment, until his paradise is shattered by the murder of his family. It is a lonely life again for Johnson after that, but he finds comfort in his fellow mountain man Del Gue, who, like the legendary Davy Crockett of the Almanacs, boasts of his accomplishments by screaming in the wilderness: "I'm half horse, half man, I got the prettiest gal, the fastest horse, the ugliest dog this side of hell; I can outrun, out-jump, throw down, drag out and whip any man," and yells out the mountain man credo: "This here is God's finest sculpture, there ain't no laws and there ain't no churches. My God, I'm a mountain man." After a final meeting with his mentor, the older mountain man Bear Claw, Johnson heads up to Canada, where "I hear there's land a man has never seen." The man who has learnt to survive in the wilderness, and has become almost as savage as the Indians, finds spiritual solace in the untouched beauty of a virgin land.

This is a concept that has been part of the mythology of the West from the beginning. Jeremiah Johnson belongs to a long line of frontiersmen, such as Davy Crockett and Daniel Boone, who built the American national identity by bridging the difference between the natural life of the Indians and the civilized traditions of the Europeans, and eventually became the cowboys, gunfighters, outlaws and lawmen of western lore. Rita Parks says: "The European became the frontiersman or the Daniel Boone. Moving deeper into the wilderness as scout, hunter, or trapper, he became the mountain man or the Kit Carson. Warring with the Spaniards and Indians in the Southwest and pointing his herds north from Texas he became the lawman, the gunman, or the cowboy—each with his real-life counterpart in men like Wyatt Earp or James Butler Hickock or William Bonney."[15]

One of the earliest literary embodiments of this figure is Hawkeye, the white man raised by Indians created by James Fenimore Cooper in *The Last of the Mohicans* (1826), a novel written at a time when the white settlers had to find ways to justify their treatment of the Native Americans. His story was turned into many films, the most famous starring Randolph Scott in 1936, and it was reworked through a modern sensibility in *The Last of the Mohicans* (1992) directed by Michael Mann starring Daniel Day Lewis. Each generation of Americans seems to be reinterpreting their western history in order to justify its present ideology and reinvent its future.

In the late 1960s early 1970s the Vietnam War, the civil rights movement and the Republican presidency of Richard Nixon influenced films like *Jeremiah Johnson* that glorified anti-war sentiments and a peaceful coexistence with the racially different Indians. As Lenihan says, "Westerns during the latter half of the sixties and early seventies conveyed a more critical and fatalistic view of a violence-prone nation that was contributing to prolonged and ultimately meaningless wars." Almost like a draft dodger from the 1960s, "the legendary trapper of *Jeremiah Johnson* prefers the natural hazards of the wilderness to fighting for his country in the Mexican War." Eventually "the social dropout turned mountain man in *Jeremiah Johnson* discovers that the Indian cruelties he has suffered are part of nature's way in a raw wilderness where beauty and savagery are inseparable."[16]

In the 1990s the popular media discovered that the traditional Turner frontier thesis was no longer used by New Western Historians as a workable explanation for the development of American society; and this awareness produced a number of revisionist Westerns, such as *Dances with Wolves* (1990) by Kevin Costner, *Unforgiven* (1992) by Clint Eastwood, *Posse* (1993) by Mario Van Peebles, *Tombstone* (1993) by George Cosmatos, *Wyatt Earp* (1994) by Lawrence Kasdan, *Geronimo: An American Legend* (1994) by Walter Hill, *Bad Girls* (1994) by Jonathan Kaplan, *The Ballad of Little Joe* (1994) by Maggie Greenwald, *The Quick and the Dead* (1994) by Sam Raimi, *Maverick* (1994) by Richard Donner, *Wild Bill* (1995) by Walter Hill, *Hi-Lo Country* (1999) by Stephen Frears.

Richard White, in organizing an exhibition at the Newberry Library in 1991, contrasted Turner's thesis, about the white man's advancing civilization in a wilderness that was largely uninhabited, with Buffalo Bill's Wild West Show, whose underlying philosophy emphasized the white man's Manifest Destiny in conquering a land teeming with hostile Indians. Both narratives, though, are gendered as male and told from a white man's perspective, and "in lamenting the lost frontier, the primitive and direct combat with nature,"[17] Turner and Buffalo Bill worried about a loss of manhood; they saw the frontier as masculine, cities and machines as feminine. This Anglo-Saxon male point of view despises and marginalizes non-whites, immigrants, and women, while New Western History seeks to portray an experience that is more varied and complicated. Patricia Limerick points out that to use the term "frontier" as "a synonym for the American Nation's westward movement," cannot "do justice to the prior presence of Indian people, to the northward movement of Spanish-speaking people, or the eastward movement of Asians."[18] English-speaking white men were the stars of Turner's narrative, says Limerick, "Indians, Hispanics, French Canadians, and Asian were at best supporting actors and at worst invisible. Nearly as invisible were women of all ethnicities."[19] Today, "because of feminism's insistence since the late 60s that women be recognized as active players in all facets of society, women have become an essential part of the western story, as have ethnic and racial groups."[20]

A recent example of this changed perspective is *The Missing* (2003) directed by Ron Howard from the 1995 novel *The Last Ride* by Tom Eidson, where the western hero is a woman (Cate Blanchett). Maggie Gilkeson gets on her horse with a rifle to chase after bad Indians who have kidnapped her teenage daughter (Evan Rachel Wood); she reluctantly accepts the help of her estranged father (Tommy Lee Jones), who years before had "gone Indian" and left the family to paint the native tribes that fascinated him. They join up with a Chirikaua chief and his son, whose bride was also kidnapped, to go after a savage *brujo* who employs black magic to put a curse on Maggie; only by knowing the Indian beliefs and their spiritual chants can this spell be broken. This narrative shows that the western woman, who already knows about medicine as a healer, but previously had disdain for the native culture, has to rely on knowledge of the Indian ways to survive, defeat the rogue Indian scouts with the help of friendly Indians who are her equals in humanity. Cate Blanchett explains her character's transformation: "I read a lot of diaries of the journeys made by the women West and the interactions with Native American, but it was important to me that Maggie wasn't a noble heroine. Because of the fact that her father had left the family and had gone native, probably hadn't had particularly good experiences with the Native Americans, she blamed them in a strange way for every misfortune that had happened in her life. I found that kind of racism through fear is an interesting place for her to start; and therefore, when she begins to understand where Jones is coming from, it gave her a more open perspective on things."[21]

In 1972, the early days of the feminist movement, Redford and Pollack in *Jeremiah Johnson* presented a relationship between the white frontiersman and the Indian woman that was more realistic and less idealized than in earlier Westerns. Johnson's squaw is not a pure young girl who inspires feelings of romantic love in the hero, like Debra Paget does to Jimmy Stewart in *Broken Arrow* (1950), or a beautiful proud warrior like the Indian Princess whom Kirk Douglas and his buddy both desire in *The Big Sky* (1952); Swan is plain and the hero didn't want her at first, but learns to love her in time. This is a primitive relationship, though, not a modern one, and the female does not talk back to the male. Prats says, "The mythology . . . has almost always identified 'the Indian' as male. The male Indian is the 'Savage' who blocks the white nation's way to the fulfillment of its exalted destiny, the enemy whose powers the hero must appropriate in order to defeat him, the primal sexual force that must be kept from the white woman. How would the New World tell its tales without La Malinche in 1520 or Pocahontas in 1607 or Sacagawea in 1804? Yet, despite the instrumental, even essential, presence of the Indian woman in the chronicles of . . . Conquest, she features far less prominently in the Western. She can be the exotic bride of a white renegade and, of course, . . . she must be the chief's daughter, the fabled 'Indian Princess.' In the mythology of the Frontier, this Indian woman is at least as . . . memorable as *Jeremiah Johnson*'s Swan."[22]

In the intervening years the importance of the Indian woman in enlightening the western man about the virtues of Indian civilization has been recognized. In *Dances with Wolves* (1990) Lt Dunbar (Kevin Costner) learns to communicate with the Indians through a squaw, Stands with Fists (Mary McDonnell); even though she is a white woman raised by the Sioux since childhood who rediscovers her forgotten English to communicate with the hero. In *The New World* (2005) by Terence Malick, Pocahontas, Chief Powhatan's favorite daughter, learns English from Captain Smith (Colin Farrell); in turn the white man comes to appreciate the playful and innocent lifestyle of the Naturals: "They are gentle, loving, faithful, lacking in all guile and trickery. They have no jealousy, no sense of possession."

Pollack spent many nights up in Utah talking to Redford about the special personal significance of this film for them and the feelings they wanted to express with it, such as "the mystique of the mountain, the sense of being alone on those mountains, the gradual learning to survive and support yourself and exist in the wilderness, with only your hands and a few simple tools."[23] He says that this kind of primitive existence is appealing to people who live in a modern world that has become too technological. "There is an immense nostalgia for the simplicity and clarity of a world in which the only way you suffer is when nature or external circumstances impose suffering on you, because that's dealable in a way that's much simpler than psychological problems. So it's appealing to everybody who's caught up in this high-tech, super-civilized, ultra-modern mechanized world. Life had a simplicity when your goal was to make enough money, or jerky, or beans, or salt or whatever to survive for a while, and then find a warm place to be, and get some skin to cover you and maybe find a woman. There's something primitive in the appeal of that kind of self-reliance. That's why we had a great time with the cabin building and all of that, like trying to build a fire, making a flinthead, or finding the right berries to eat; life was reduced to absolute essentials, and there's a comforting clarity about it that doesn't exist today."[24]

A long tradition in American literature portrayed the western hero as "a skillful man, both physically and mentally. He handles tools well, whether they are equipment or weapons. He is at home with nature—the desolate terrain of mountains and deserts, the raging fury of treacherous streams, the awesome storms of rain, snow, dust, and wind."[25]

In traditional western iconography the cabin always had a central place: "A cabin, built with simple tools from local materials, proclaimed self-reliance and a connection with place."[26] It stressed the courage of the builder and represented progress; the presence of a woman often signified the intention of the hunter to settle down into family life and start farming. This is the meaning, for example, of the cabin and cornfield in *Apache* (1954), where Burt Lancaster as the Indian warrior Massai eventually renounces his relentless struggle with the white man when his woman becomes pregnant. In *Jeremiah Johnson* Swan is not pregnant, as she is in Fisher's book *Mountain Man*; there is an adopted son and a family unit, but the mountain man has not given up hunting. Like the Indians, he does not want to turn the wilderness into a garden, only survive in a natural primitive state; the murder of his family sends him back alone and homeless to wonder into the mountains.

The longing for a simpler more spiritual existence in nature, as opposed to the complicated and technological modern world, is a constant theme in Redford's films, from *Jeremiah Johnson* to *Electric Horseman* both directed by Sydney Pollack, from *A River Runs Through It* to *The Horse Whisperer* directed by Redford himself. That's how Pollack explains its significance: "It's kind of simplistic to say it but it's true, the more advanced we get scientifically, technologically, the farther we get from nature. It's the reason that parks and wildlife areas become so precious now, because we see it on the verge of extinction; and so it's become desperately important, it's a preoccupation with everybody. We're saturated with cities and cars, high speed trains, high speed jets, computers and information; so there's a theory, a feeling that you have to spend at least some of your time around something that's more impressive or bigger or better than anything a man can make, whether it's a mountain, or the sea, or the sky, or something. The idea is that there are lessons to be learned from it, but more importantly that there's a stabilizing influence it gives your psyche; you get a balance that you don't get when all you can see is a building, or a computer screen, or cars, or trains, or something."[27]

In Turner's view progress was also achieved "by retreating to the primitive along successive frontiers. Being in continuous touch with the simplicity of primitive societies shaped the American character."[28] Since the early 1800s the myth-makers of the American West "developed two themes: the general theme of the wilderness versus civilization, and the more personal notion of the desire on the part of the over-civilized to escape back to nature and the original harmony enjoyed by innocent savages."[29]

This idea of protecting the natural environment as a means of spiritual solace does not only apply to the American West but to the rest of the world; it was the subtext of another film that Pollack directed starring Redford, *Out Of Africa*. Pollack says that Kenya really felt like a Garden of Eden, when he was shooting the film there in 1985, but it had already been ruined by civilization. "There was a sense that it was over then, and now it really breaks my heart, because I love Africa, and those plains are all rotted up with car tracks and wastepaper. It's not going to be there anymore, it's tragic. That's why there's such hell going on about endangered species, wild life preservation and all of this, because, as civilization keeps going, it's just swallowing it all; and it's kind of terrifying to think what's going to happen in a couple of hundred years."[30]

For Redford and for Pollack the message of preservation of the natural environment does not simply have a connotation of nostalgia for a past that is gone and forever lost, but it also serves as an impetus to be active and committed in a concrete way in today's world. It comes from a liberal and progressive political stance, not a conservative male-chauvinist ideology, as in the films by Clint Eastwood, Sam Peckinpah, John Milius and Walter Hill.

5. THE ELECTRIC HORSEMAN

The cowboy defies the corporation

Redford and Pollack explore the conflict between the values of individual freedom in a contemporary society dominated by greedy corporations in the modern Western *The Electric Horseman* (1979). This film represents a departure from the pessimistic Westerns that, since the 1960s, had lamented the end of an anachronistic way of life on the open range, from *The Misfits* (1961) to *The Wild Bunch* (1969). John Lenihan says that by 1963 Westerns "had begun to depict the modern urban civilization as empty and dehumanizing in contrast with the dying frontier world of the freedom-loving individualists. Cowboys, adventurers, and lawmen who once found fulfillment as self-sufficient individuals became forgotten anachronisms, as an institutionalized, confining urban order replaced the open frontier."[1] Pollack says he was tired of such guilty self-examination and wanted to make a fairy-tale Western with an optimistic ending, where the disillusioned cowboy, through the love for his horse, rediscovers his true self in the simplicity of nature. Redford worked closely with the director on this purposefully light-hearted film, before embarking in the socially committed *Brubaker* (1979) and his dramatic directorial debut, *Ordinary People* (1980).

In *The Electric Horseman* Redford plays Sonny Steele, a former rodeo rider who has won the title of "All around world champion cowboy" five times in a row and has the broken bones, trophies, and brass belt buckles to prove it. A montage over the opening credits shows his past glories, and his current occupation as a walking advertisement for a cereal company. His image is on billboards and life-size cutouts, like the Marlboro Man; he is promoted as a living symbol of the Wild West to sell Ranch Breakfast to the children of America.

Steele is a shadow of his former self. He's a drunk, a womanizer, he falls off his horse, can't remember his lines; he's a man who's lost, but doesn't seem to know what's wrong. He tells his old roadies, who now work for him, that their present life beats the rodeo circuit; now they drive around in a white Cadillac convertible, fly first class, stay in fancy hotels with room service: "We're living like a bunch of oil barons." It's clear that Sonny Steele has sold out his integrity for money and it's eating away at his conscience.

Willie Nelson, the Country and Western singer who plays Steele's manager, joins the others in singing one of the songs he recorded for the soundtrack, as a humorous comment on the tough life of a cowboy: "Mama don't let your babies grow up to be cowboys. Don't let them pick guitars and drive in old trucks, make 'em be doctors and lawyers and such. Mamas don't let your babies grow up to be cowboys. They'll never stay home and they're always alone, even with someone they love." Many years later—when Redford was awarded the Kennedy Center Honor in 2005—Nelson would pay tribute to his old friend with another song from the soundtrack, "My Heroes Have Always Been Cowboys."

In situating this film in a line of 1960s and 1970s Westerns that dealt powerfully "with the end of the West, the passing of its heroic and mythical age and its entry into the modern world of cities and technology," Cawelti says that "the sense of the myth's archaism is even stronger in a recent film like The Electric Horseman where the protagonist is deeply concerned that he has become nothing more than a shadowy image of a ghostly past."[2]

Sonny Steele is about to make a public appearance at Las Vegas Caesars Palace in his neon-lit cowboy suit on a new thoroughbred horse, Rising Star—that the cereal company has bought for $12 million—when he realizes that the animal has been shot full of tranquilizers, steroids that will make him sick and sterile. Steele tries to complain about the treatment of the horse to the company's CEO, but he is reminded that nobody forced him to take on this simple job, which has made him more rich and famous than he ever was. Witnessing the suffering of the horse and understanding his own complicity is a wake-up call for Steele's conscience; he calmly decides to ride Rising Star right out of the casino, through the neon-lit city at night, all the way to the Nevada desert wilderness. He rides from Las Vegas, an artificial city that is symbolic of American materialism, towards the personal freedom that can only be found in nature.

With this portrayal of a beleaguered cowboy Redford is probably also representing his own desire to escape from the media circus that has invaded his personal life because of his celebrity. The bad guys of the piece are not only the company men and the enforcers—the local police; another pursuer is a woman who represents the corporate-owned media.

An enterprising television news journalist, Hallie Martin (Jane Fonda), is clever enough to figure out where Steele is going and follow him; when she catches up to him and asks him to give her a story, he's uncooperative; he doesn't want to be on television. She tries to convince him of the importance of informing the public: "Everybody wants to know the truth about the great American cowboy and the world champion horse riding together into the sunset," to which he replies, "Why, are you full of shit!" But when the AMPCO Corporation tries to discredit the cowboy by announcing that "Steele has a long history of drug and alcohol abuse," he decides to set the record straight and agrees to be interviewed on camera.

This plot twist reflects Redford's ambivalent attitude towards the media; he's adamant about wanting to preserve his privacy and avoid the spotlight for himself, but he understands the value of journalists as watchdogs, a corrective to the power of politicians, as he demonstrated by producing *All the President's Men* (1976).

When the newswoman meets the cowboy, she's carrying a video camera on a tripod while wearing tight jeans and high-heel boots; when she trips and falls, she jokes: "I think I've broken my leg, what are you going to do? Shoot me?" This is an insider's reference *They Shoot Horses, Don't They?* (1970) also directed by Sydney Pollack. In that film Jane Fonda played a desperate woman during the Depression who decides she doesn't want to live—while engaged in an exhausting dance marathon—and convinces her partner to shoot her, just like one would do with an injured horse.

"I'm not used to being talked about as a horse thief," Steele explains, making reference to the common western outlaw practice of horse rustling or mavericking. He might have stolen the horse, but it's for its own good. He respects Rising Star, "This horse is a champion. He's got more heart, more drive and more soul than most people you'll ever know," and believes he's defending the "human" rights of the horse, "Maybe they bought him, maybe they own him, but there's some rights you can't buy, even from an animal." He wants to give the horse the better life that he feels he has earned and intends to set him free in the wilderness, in the company of other wild mustangs.

Pollack explains the connection between the cowboy and his horse: "He sees himself in the horse without knowing it; he's this guy who is a champion, and he extols this horse as a champion; he doesn't have the ego or the psychological sense to stand up for himself, but underneath he identifies with that horse, with the fact that he was once something and now he's used fodder; he's been exploited by big business and by the fact that there isn't any prestige awarded that kind of individualism anymore. He's sort of swallowed up in corporate America and he sees a metaphor for himself in this horse. So he kidnaps the horse and he redeems himself; by letting the horse go free he's gotten himself free of the AMPCO Corporation and all of that in some way."[3]

After stealing the horse Steele is headed for a canyon in Utah, driving the camper borrowed from a friend, while the police is searching for him; when he's trapped in a road block, he decides to escape by riding off on the horse where police cars and motorcycles can't follow him. The extended chase is humorous and meant to juxtapose visually the limber image of the fast riding cowboy to the clumsy machinery of civilized society. The symbolic meaning is clear; as Jane Tompkins points out in *West of Everything*, horses are the heart and soul of the Western, they "fulfill a longing for a different kind of existence. Anti-modern, anti-urban, anti-technological, they stand for an existence without cars and telephones and electricity."[4] It's the same idea that was at the core of *Jeremiah Johnson*: the appeal of nature, symbolized here by the horse, for people living in a society that has become too technological for human beings.

In *Electric Horseman* the cowboy hero has a love relationship with a woman who's out of touch with nature and her inner self. Pollack says: "She represents the world that's doing the exploiting, she is the emissary from the corporate world and she is the opposite of personal experience, while he is the epitome of personal experience. He goes through everything, she watches and writes about it. They are two completely different kinds of people, which is why they can't be together in the end. She doesn't have anything to do, unless something bad happens to somebody else; she's a reporter who just waits for something to report on. I don't mean that real reporters are like that, but those are the prototypes or the archetypes that we used for the sake of the movie."[5]

Eventually the TV journalist convinces Steele to let her tag along, even when he has to continue on foot, and much fun is made of this foolish city woman stumbling along in her high heels, while carrying heavy camera equipment. In the wilderness the cowboy is the competent one; just like Jeremiah Johnson, Sonny Steele knows how to cook food for himself, build a campfire, sleep outdoors, take care of the horse. Tompkins explains: "Far from town, far from the conveniences of modern life, far from outside help, the solitary man, with only nature at his disposal, makes himself comfortable."[6] She theorizes that the land is almost like a woman for the western hero, who finds comfort in lying down with her at night. In these modern Westerns, there is also a real woman with the hero around the campfire—the Indian wife Swan in *Jeremiah Johnson* and the reporter in *Electric Horseman*—and he beds down with her, making the connection between Mother Nature and female energy as a place of comfort for the male.

The man and the woman in *Electric Horseman* are attracted by their differences. While Martin admires the cowboy's ease in the natural setting, Steele is impressed by her competence on the job; when she calls him Norman, his real name, he compliments her for having done her homework. He then finds out that her given name is Alice and a new sense of intimacy is created between them. It's her determination, as well as her vulnerability as a New York City woman who's quite helpless in the wild, that eventually melts the hardened cowboy's heart. The morning after their first sexual encounter, she's nervous and he has to remind her that what happened between them the night before is not going to be on television; just to make sure of that, Steele throws her camera cases in the river. He doesn't know that she has already alerted the network to send a camera crew to Rim Rock Canyon, the place where she believes Steele is going to release the horse, although now she regrets having betrayed him.

Gradually the woman will stop reporting on events and begin to live life. When Steele inquires about her note-taking—as they walk through the beautiful natural scenery, under the open sky and colorful sunsets, and she learns about the land from the cowboy—the reporter reads what she has written: "I feel I'm seeing this country for the first time." She is now convinced of the righteousness of this man's cause, and confesses her betrayal during their last night together in an abandoned outlaw cabin. The joke is on her, when the next morning she finds out that they're going to another location, Silver Reef, to meet the wild stallions. All ends well when the AMPCO executives decide not to press charges, after realizing that the media attention has increased cereal sales and that people see Steele as a hero fighting against evil corporate guys who have mistreated an innocent animal.

Before releasing him Steele talks to Rising Star and reminds him that those wild animals are horses just like him, and it's in his blood to hold his own among them. Redford is already a man who can talk to horses in this film, as in *The Horse Whisperer* (1998), which he would direct many years later. In *Lonely Are the Brave* (1962)—a modern Western that has been compared to *The Electric Horseman*, but has a pessimistic rather than an optimistic tone—Kirk Douglas and his horse Whiskey eventually get hit by a truck, as if the film were saying that it is civilization that killed the western heroes and their horses, the representatives of a free way of life doomed to extinction. In *The Horse Whisperer* the initial tragedy is provoked by a big rig skidding out of control on a mountain road, killing a horse and a young rider, leaving another girl injured and her horse spooked. But the horse is not put down, as everybody thinks he should be; he's brought to the horse whisperer to be healed and in the process his owner and her mother are also healed. Therefore we see Redford continuing with the theme that contact with nature and wild animals can have a spiritually healing effect on modern men, and women. It is a message of hopeful optimism.

Sydney Pollack says that this was their intention in making a film like *Electric Horseman*, that the original screenplay was dated with the "attitudes of the 60's, serious, psychedelic and very anti-corporation."[7] The director collaborated with Redford in turning the script into an old-fashioned movie, like Frank Capra's *Mr Deeds Goes to Town* (1936) or *It Happened One Night* (1934). "We realized that something innocent and marvelous had been lost from the movies. We wondered why not make a picture like that now, full of fantasy and optimism and good feelings. We tried to make a fairy tale where you root for virtue and evil gets its comeuppance."[8] That's why *Electric Horseman* has been defined by some critics a fantasy Western. Pollack agrees, "It's a kind of contemporary Western, in the sense that it takes place in the outdoors and it has the tools and the props that a Western has, campfires, horses, canteens, guns; but it's more of a romantic comedy."[9]

As to what attracted Redford and himself to this optimistic Western at this time, Pollack says: "The sixties and seventies have been two decades of real breast-beating and exposing of our national guilts. The focus of our films has been to examine publicly our mistakes; mistakes in urban development, mistakes in Watergate, mistakes in Vietnam, mistakes in nuclear power plants. All of which was good and healthy and right at the time. But we've had twenty years of it now and I think there is not just a need but a desperation to find positive moral values again, something to hope for, something larger than life to believe in. Spirit, heroism, patriotism, morality, anything. I think it's the reason we're in this giant swing towards Country and Western; it has to do with grassroots Americana, the desire to get back to what we invented and what we do better than anybody, which is being cowboys and ride horses and sing country songs and barbecue chicken and ribs and all that down-home stuff. You now have a plethora of western films or films with a western theme and it has to do with heroism and with wanting to find something that's American that's positive."[10]

In fact, what happened then is that the Western nearly disappeared for more than a decade and resurfaced again in the 1990s, with *Dances with Wolves* (1990) directed by Kevin Costner, a film that reverses the traditional western roles by making the Indians the innocents and the cavalry the brutal killers; and *Unforgiven* (1992) directed by Clint Eastwood, that questions the addiction to violence of western males, outlaws and marshals alike. This brief resurgence produced interesting reworkings of the genre with a new sensibility, films like *Maverick* (1994) directed by Richard Donner from a screenplay by William Goldman, that has some similarities with *Butch Cassidy and the Sundance Kid* as a comic Western based on the interplay between two gambling con men (Mel Gibson and James Garner) and a woman who loves them and tricks them both (Jodie Foster). *Wyatt Earp*

(1994), produced by Kevin Costner and directed by Lawrence Kasdan, examines from a modern perspective the life story of a marshal who has a macho attitude towards women and a tendency to resolve conflicts through violence. *The Ballad of Little Joe* (1994), written and directed by Maggie Greenwald and based on a true story, is a Western made from a woman's perspective that illustrates the sexual discrimination women were subject to in the West, which was similar to the racial prejudice against blacks or Asians. *Wild Bill* (1994), written and directed by Walter Hill, is a brooding and somber film about the psychological effects of a life of violence on a western hero (Jeff Bridges) and its close connection with a sense of impending death.

It appears that the revisionist Westerns of the 1960s and 1970s prefigured themes that will be addressed with an increased awareness in the 1990s. Rita Parks says that, because the contemporary Western "takes place at a moment when the frontiers of both time and place are but a memory, the frontier is located in the character's frustrated nostalgia or in a world view that is basically anachronistic and out of touch with contemporary life." But the value of these stories is that they "frequently refer to the past as a comment upon the present."[11]

The Western seems out of favor again today (at least on the big screen, while it's still popular on television), after a few years of interesting revisionism in the 1990s, but the enduring fascination with the American West remains part of the national consciousness and a mythology that is forever fascinating for Europeans who haven't had this experience in their recent past. This is how Pollack explains it: "The American West has become a symbol for what it was, because it was the last frontier to be conquered. You Europeans did it too, but you did it so long ago; I mean, there were frontiers in Europe too, but they were before people were taking pictures of it and all of that stuff, so it didn't get reported in the same way. But we were the youngest of the countries, so our past, our origins are so recent, a couple of hundred years, that everything was archetypal in the West. There was bad nature, there was good nature, there were the tidal waves and the winds and the cold, and there was the sun; there were Indians that were going to try to kill you, there were bears that would try to eat you, there were heroic guys in white hats with guns who could shoot. It was all very much like a morality play, it was so simple, good and evil; it was absolutely mythical in a way, except it was the truth, it's what happened. So it has held a fascination not just for Americans but for Europeans too; Westerns are popular in Europe."[12]

John Cawelti had noticed in *The Six-Gun Mystique* (1984) that international interest—French, German, Italian and Japanese—in the mythical forms of the Western had been stronger than in America since 1970. Pollack was addressing his comments about Europeans' fascination with the Western to me, because he knew I was born in Italy. As an Italian woman who became an American citizen later in life, I have a keen interest in the West, because this is where the American identity was formed, and a cultural curiosity for a mythology that is so thoroughly male, but has been interiorized by men, women and children of all nationalities. Like millions of children around the world I played at Cowboys and Indians—with toy bows and arrows and Winchester rifles, riding a broom as my horse—and dreamed of traveling to America to meet up with my western screen heroes. An American woman like Rita Parks says that the Man of the West "represents those qualities of pioneer spirit, initiative, skill, and daring that we Americans have always wanted to believe are uniquely our own."[13] Robert Redford has embodied these qualities in his screen persona and in his own life, therefore he's an interesting subject for a critical study that connects his work to the American West.

6. REDFORD AND POLLACK

The actor as *auteur*

Given that Sydney Pollack was directing Redford for the fifth time in *Electric Horseman*, this is the place to add a few considerations about the director's personal and professional relationship with the actor. I also use this as an illustration of the fact that Redford should be considered an *auteur* in his film career, which, for the most part, has followed a coherent and consistent path, from actor to producer then director.

James Cagney had said: "Good acting is thinking, and unless there is some intelligence behind the picture, some imagination and sincerity, you have nothing."[1] Patrick McGilligan, in his book on Cagney subtitled *The Actor As Auteur*, about the artistic influence of the performer, says, "Only actor 'poets' such as Chaplin and Buster Keaton, who wrote, directed and starred in their own films, are accorded widespread recognition as 'auteurs' artists of the first rank," but "an actor may influence a film as much as a writer, director or producer," when "he or she changes lines, adlibs, shifts meaning, influences the narrative and style of a film."[2] Cagney, who had his own production company from the 1930s to the 1950s, was able to "express a clear and personal life vision," particularly in his own independent films.

Similarly Redford started producing his own films early on and eventually moved into directing, while continuing his acting career. Perhaps not coincidentally he was thinking about Jimmy Cagney and the 1930s while making *The Sting* (1973): "The Thirties were a combination of hope and depression that produced a lot of energy, and Cagney symbolized that for me. Cagney is probably my favorite performer of all time."[3] We have to remember that in the 1960s and 1970s movie stars were not as powerful in the Hollywood film industry as they have become since then, although some of them already produced their own films in the 1950s, like Kirk Douglas and Burt Lancaster. Now many actors have tried their hand at directing, and have learnt how to take into account the larger picture; conversely directors have become less dictatorial and more receptive of the actors' input in the dialogue and the playing of scenes. It has become commonplace for studios to offer production deals to their major stars and help them set up independent companies on the lot to develop their own material. The top money earners, such as a Harrison Ford or a Tom Cruise, are consulted about everything from script to casting to the advertising campaign, even though that trend has started to reverse lately, as the 2006 break-up between Paramount and Cruise's company has demonstrated. But this was not a common occurrence in the 1960s, when Redford started acting in films; so it's remarkable that, from the very beginning, he tried to develop and produce his own projects. After being sued by Paramount for refusing to act in a Western called *Blue*, because he didn't like the changes that had been made in the script, Redford, who had tried to convince the studio to finance a film about an Olympic skier, set up his own production company, Wildwood Enterprises, for that purpose and made *Downhill Racer* (1969).

Redford had met Pollack when they were both acting in his first film, *War Hunt* (1962), then worked with him as director in *This Property is Condemned* (1966) with Natalie Wood—a tragic love story set in the South during the Depression—and they had become friends. When Redford couldn't return the $200,000 advance the studio had paid him to star in *Jeremiah Johnson,* because, says Pollack, "Sundance was eating up every nickel that he had. He was broke," the director had to personally guarantee to Warner Bros that he could shoot the film on location in Utah, for the same budget that it would cost to do it on the back-lot; and if they went over, the money would have to come out of their pocket. Pollack says, "We were in a terrible jam and what ensued was a real testing of our friendship."[4]

After their bonding experience in Utah, Pollack convinced Redford to accept the role of Hubbell Gardiner opposite Barbra Streisand in *The Way*

We Were (1973): "We needed someone strong enough to counter-balance Barbra. She'd been running all over her leading men."[5] Redford hated this weak golden boy, who let himself be seduced by the easy life of money and privilege in Hollywood during the McCarthy era, while his wife was a Jewish activist committed to liberal causes: "In the original script the character was passive all the way through, he was just there for her to love as an object."[6] But because he had a creative collaboration with the director, Redford was confident that Pollack would let him add some complex dimensions to make the character more interesting: "Here was a guy who just had to stand around and be attractive enough for her to fall in love with him. I said there have to be some underpinnings that at least suggest a darker side. The darker side here is that he has not written a great novel. He doesn't want to be put up on that pedestal. And there's a certain grace in just knowing that."[7]

Pollack also directed Redford in the political thriller *Three Days of the Condor* (1975) with Faye Dunaway, from the novel by James Grady *Six Days of the Condor*, about a CIA reader whose life is in danger when he discovers an unauthorized intelligence system within the agency. Redford will explore the theme of covert government operations in *All The President's Men* (1976), directed by Alan Pakula, about the *Washington Post* investigative reporters Bob Woodward and Carl Bernstein, who uncovered the Watergate scandal and eventually caused Richard Nixon to resign.

Pollack directed Redford again in *Out of Africa* (1986) with Meryl Streep, about the real-life love story between Karen Blixen (Danish writer Isak Dinesen), a strong independent woman, and Denys Finch Hatton, an English safari hunter in Kenya who wants to maintain his freedom in the relationship. Then Pollack directed Redford in *Havana* (1990) with Lena Olin, another love story, set in Cuba at the eve of the Castro revolution, between a cynical gambler and a woman with strong political beliefs.

The director said about his special relationship with the actor: "In some ways we are very different; I tend to be over-organized, and maybe I drive him a little crazy, while he tends to be disorganized; but in the ways that are most important for any kind of collaboration, like taste or judgment of a scene, we are very similar, so in that sense we have had a very good working relationship for 25 years. There are two areas to our relationship, one is professional and one is personal; we happen to be fairly close friends and have been for a long time, so we have a degree of comfort with each other that makes things easier. Trying to be creative is an intimate act, and it's hard to do that with strangers; that's why people often work with people they're familiar with, there's something economical emotionally about it. So it's easy for me to direct Bob, he takes direction well, and I would say that he trusts me enough to just be an actor when he works. The fact that he has directed doesn't really affect the way we work together; for the first five films that we made he had not been a director, but afterwards nothing changed; honestly I haven't noticed any difference, he's the same . . . just as difficult as ever!"[8]

Pollack confesses to a type of identification between Redford and himself, which is evident in their demeanor: the two friends wear the same jeans, the same cowboy boots and western shirts, they spend winter holidays together in Sundance, where Pollack built a home next to Redford's. "In some ways he's been the alter ego for me in all of the films I've made. I believe in some ways he's played the same character. I've sort of watched that guy grow up and get older and come to the end of the line in a way in *Havana*. It's one of the reasons I'm so attached to *Havana*, because in my opinion that's the same guy that started out in *This Property is Condemned* and went through *The Way We Were* and *Jeremiah Johnson*, *Three Days of the Condor*, *The Electric Horseman* and so on. He's really essentially this unpossessable, unattached individualist, who believes there's some utopian way for him not to have to bend to the needs of a structured society and not to have to give up any of himself in order to either have a relationship or a sense of community, and finds that neither is possible. Except now he's aging, and he's no longer a young, handsome guy where that can paper over a lot of the hard knocks of being alone. That's been a journey that we've made since 1965 together, when I first directed him."[9]

Because of their long collaboration Pollack has an informed opinion of Redford's qualities as an actor, "Redford sometimes gets attacked for not messing himself up more in parts, but he's not a character actor, like Paul Muni was; you don't want to see him shave his head, put on a pot belly and have two teeth missing; nobody wants to see Redford do that. I like to see Dustin Hoffman do it, or Jack Nicholson, but not somebody like Gary Cooper; he's just a different kind of an actor. You want Redford to be a hero, that's the way he's most fulfilling for the audience."[10]

Pollack believes Redford is also a good actor, not simply a movie star, although different from somebody like Dustin Hoffman. "I believe Redford withholds. Part of the attraction to Redford is that you keep wanting to go back and see what there is that you missed the first time. There's something mysterious about Redford. You have the feeling that, if he had ten dollars, five of it stays in his pocket. I mean, he would give you five dollars, but he's not giving you everything; and that, I think, is a great deal of his appeal. Dustin, on the other hand, spends all ten dollars, he shows you everything that's going on, he's a very generous actor in a different kind of way. It's true that Redford is more of a conventional movie star, but I think his acting is just as good, only his style is different, he's a withholder."[11]

As a restrained and controlled actor, Redford is capable of suggesting a darker undercurrent behind the handsome exterior of his golden boy good looks in films like *The Way We Were* and *The Great Gatsby*. He explored a similar theme in his first film as director, *Ordinary People* (1980), based on the 1976 novel by Judith Guest, which is about an adolescent (Timothy Hutton) from a perfect middle-class family, who's suicidal and finds himself in trouble psychologically, because there was too much emotional withholding on the part of his family, particularly his mother (Mary Tyler Moore). Redford explains the connection with his own life, where it was his father who was emotionally distant, not his mother: "I had very strong feelings about the material and particularly one character, that I had seen all my life but never on film, that cannot get in touch with her feelings and needs to pretend that everything is okay when it's not, and the consequence of that on people around them. So that was the heart of the attraction for me, to work with something that I had never seen on film, but I seemed to be surrounded by in my life and it bothered me."[12]

Redford would deal with the same subject again, a golden boy who cannot express to his family the darker longings of his nature, in *A River Runs Through It* (1992) with Brad Pitt, and in *The Legend of Bagger Vance* (2000) with Matt Damon as the golfing golden boy from Savannah who was undone by the tragedy of World War I. He said: "I've always been interested in community and lives where order is important, where people are concerned how others perceive them—and then to see what they do when tragedy strikes and the whole fabric begins to come apart."[13]

Redford wanted to direct, after acting and producing, to express a wider range of his artistic abilities and find a connection with his youthful aspiration to become a painter. He explains: "In making a film, you have directors and producers and editors and sound people who want to alter your performance. No question, it's a collaborative medium. I've been frustrated for many years in wanting to have total control of something. It's like doing a painting. I started out to be an artist, and the one thing I always missed as an actor was that when you painted a picture it was yours. No one came in and changed anything for you. One person doesn't make a film, ten people do. But directing comes about as close as you can get to having it exactly as you want."[14]

The acceptance of Redford's first directing effort by the Hollywood establishment was as overwhelming as that later accorded to other movie stars turned directors: Warren Beatty for *Reds* (1981), Kevin Costner for *Dances with Wolves* (1990), Mel Gibson for *Braveheart* (1995). *Ordinary People* (1980) was nominated for six Academy Awards and won four, including a Best Director Oscar for Redford. But the maverick with an outlaw western sensibility wanted to organize an alternative to Hollywood-style filmmaking and a place to learn how to make different, independent films. That's how the Sundance Institute was born in 1980. To this day Sundance remains an unqualified success in developing talent and has exported its teaching model to other countries.

7. SUNDANCE

An educational experiment in the mountains

Robert Redford set up the Sundance Institute in 1980, on the site of his Utah ski resort, in order to help inexperienced filmmakers develop their script projects into films, and the first Filmmakers Lab was held there in June 1981. In 1984 the Sundance Institute took over the U.S. Film Festival in nearby Park City, Utah—which was renamed Sundance Film Festival from January 1985—with the purpose of showcasing independent films. This annual event has become extremely important as a place for agents, studios and distributors to locate new talent: films, actors and directors. In 1996 a Sundance cable channel was launched with a program of domestic and foreign independent features and documentaries.

Redford says, "When the studios began to change in the 1980s and moving more towards special effects-oriented, more action, more blockbuster, the youth market, I felt that they might be vacating a space for the other kinds of films that I would call more humanistic. So I committed to play whatever small part I could in keeping that alive; and that's what started Sundance. So it was putting two things together, one was coming up with a mechanism, the workshops, to give an opportunity for new artists to have a place to come and work; in particular I wanted them to feel like they could fail, because I think failure can be a sign of growth rather than the end of something. And the other thing was start the festival and move it to the mountains in the middle of winter to make it hard to get to, so it would draw more attention to it and be exclusively for independent film."[1]

The stated purpose of Sundance of promoting experimental filmmaking has been achieved and Redford is satisfied. "I'm very happy that Sundance is being acknowledged, because maybe in the end this is the final reward, acknowledgement for what you tried to do. What Sundance is about is development, it's not about us being involved in the product, that's up to somebody else; our involvement is to help new people develop their skills, so that more films of a personal nature will get into the market place, and try to keep alive the idea against forces who seem to move towards a more centralized industry. A lot of the films are expensive and dependent on high technology, which is all fine, this is a broad industry that accommodates that; personally I'm interested in films that are more humanitarian in nature and deal with the complex issues that face all of our lives on a more psychological basis. So, when Sundance sponsors films, the filmmakers will be sponsored, not just the project; it pleases me to see the product arrive to festivals, get into the marketplace. That's the test."[2]

Redford had discovered this secluded location in the Wasatch Mountains in the early 1960s—after marrying Lola Van Wagoner, a Mormon from Provo—while taking a shortcut through the forest on his motorcycle, on his way to visit his mother's family in Texas. In 1961 he bought two acres of land for $500, which is all he could afford at the time—before his stage success in *Barefoot in the Park*, the Neil Simon's play directed by Mike Nichols—and built a house there with his own hands, a wooden A-frame with a huge rock fireplace. Redford loved skiing on the powdery snow of Mt. Timpanogos (12,000 feet) and he responded to the silence and natural beauty of this unspoiled place, like Jeremiah Johnson did, "I saw the landscape pretty much as the first settlers did, and it was paradise."[3] He continued to buy more land through the years, and owned 200 acres by 1968, when he decided to buy the whole canyon with four partners, because Xerox and other corporations were threatening to develop the area into small lots. "To protect the area against out-of control development . . . I purchased about 5,000 acres surrounding Sundance . . . in order to preserve it. Because it was the most incredible land I'd ever seen. Remote and untouched. But I could hear the thundering hooves of development galloping towards it."[4] This is how he explains the conflict between preserving nature and exploiting it: "We're a Manifest Destiny country, and development-oriented. It's just a question of time before we develop a way to live inside things that we create rather than living with nature."[5] So Redford bought the land to protect it from developers, but then he had to figure out a way to make the $3 million investment pay for itself; and he confesses it's been a nightmare.

In 1969, after the success of *Butch Cassidy and the Sundance Kid*, Redford started to set up a ski resort in the area, and he named it Sundance from his character in the film. Later he named the primitive restaurant at the end of the ski lifts "Bearclaw Cabin" from the name of Jeremiah Johnson's mountain man mentor. Redford also built himself an imposing solar-powered house of glass and stone nearby, that he still considers his principal residence. It's from the sanctuary of this protected enclave in the wilderness of the Rocky Mountains, an alternative to his urban New York apartment, that Redford has been conducting his life and managing his career.

The Sundance Resort, opened in 1988, consists of three clusters of ninety-five rustic cabins and cottages spread out in the forest, built of unvarnished wood and tastefully decorated in Southwestern style; there are also 170 privately owned homes hidden away further up the road, but the environmentalist Redford has stopped further development. "I wanted its structure to be rustic, almost pioneer in spirit. Sundance is a place to stay, even to live, with an enormous amount of nature to walk through. No building is over the tree line. The land is the principal thing to be observed . . . I never wanted to manage a resort. I see it as a structure that supports the creative . . . This has been like one big painting, one lifelong sculpture."[6] The neatly kept grounds are connected by foot-paths lined by colorful wildflowers and criss-crossed by murmuring brooks and waterfalls that flow into a pond which recycles the water in the central area, where a life-size bronze statue of an Indian Chief in full headdress seems engaged in a ritual dance. A tall totem pole surmounted by an eagle with wings spread out in flight is another testimonial to Redford's respect for Native American culture. Black and white photos and memorabilia from Redford's films like *Butch Cassidy* and *Electric Horseman* line the walls of the reception building, alongside western art, Indian paintings and bronze animal sculptures. The General Store sells Indian artifacts and western wear; an elegant mail-order catalogue offers Indian rugs and jewelry, Southwestern furniture and lamps. The old Tree Room is a restaurant built around a huge tree, a proof of Redford's commitment to ecological concerns and his efforts to preserve nature, while building this resort that offers skiing, hiking, horseback riding and fly-fishing in a beautiful wilderness setting.

Redford explains his intentions to develop a resort that would not destroy the natural environment, but preserve its character: "I would have loved to leave Sundance the way I found it and the way it was a hundred years ago, but that was impossible—there are no more private nature preserves. We've tried to strike a balance between guarded development and realistic preservation."[7] He adds, "The resort was established just to create a revenue stream to pay for the larger picture that's been in my mind for a long time."[8] But he wanted to "prove that you don't have to tear up the land to make money," and to reverse the procedure of "putting business at the core and bringing art in as an accouterment to attract more business. What we wanted to do was to build a core of art and culture and bring business around that."[9]

In 1978 Redford had the idea of starting a film institute at Sundance, and in 1979 sent his wife's cousin, Sterling Van Wagenen, on a mission to study similar institutions, like the American Film Institute in Los Angeles and the Eugene O'Neill Theatre Center in Waterford, Connecticut. By 1980, with public funding from the National Endowment for the Arts and private money from corporations like Sony, the Sundance Institute was formed under a board of trustees that included Sydney Pollack, screenwriter Waldo Salt, and Frank Daniel, chairman of the Film Department at Columbia University and later professor at USC Film School, who became the artistic director.

Redford had never much liked school and book learning, "I never learned as much in the classroom as I did staring out a window and imagining things,"[10] so he didn't want his labs to be like a film school where professors lecture, but a place to exchange ideas that was work-oriented. "I wanted them to be educational, without a classroom, without lectures but with experienced people—writers, actors, directors, cinematographers, editors—working closely with novices. I wanted to develop a friendly atmosphere for new voices—for playwrights and moviemakers—and to preserve the art of storytelling." Frank Daniel said, "After talent, the most important thing here is that you really have to want to make movies."[11] When the first Filmmakers Lab was set up in 1981, the participants were selected on the basis of a script that they already had written and wanted to make into a movie. Redford says: "The thing we're really about at Sundance is developing skills with people who already have a project and idea, and develop it fully without losing their vision. They also get experience in using the tools of the trade."[12] His intention was to create some mechanism to help independent filmmakers along the "laborious process of getting a film made, which sometimes takes anywhere from two to four years, because they don't have the experience, it's not available to them. There's no training ground or rehearsal for film. It's just too costly."[13]

According to Michelle Satter, director of the Sundance Institute Feature Film Program, the ideal workshop candidate is someone who already has been to film school for a couple of years and has made a short film, and now wants to work on a script for a feature. Once his or her project is selected by the Sundance staff—that whittles down the 750 to 1000 applications to 20 or 25—and approved by a rotating selection committee, the full circle of the Sundance experience starts at the Screenwriters Lab in January and continues at the Directors Lab in June, where actual scenes are shot and edited with state-of-the-art video equipment and the help of small crews of technical support people and actors. The script is examined again, from a more practical point of view, during a second Screenwriters Lab at the end of June; then the filmmaker might be invited to the Independent Producers Conference in August, to discuss the possibilities of the marketplace. Some of the projects are actually developed into films, and Sundance is ready to help by suggesting agents and financing venues; when the film is then completed, it might be selected for presentation at the Sundance Film Festival, where a distributor could be secured. Redford says: "Ideally, it would be nice if Sundance could create a situation where a filmmaker could come with his or her product and work it through the process that we provide here, which is an exact replica of the filmmaking process from the very beginning of script development right to the end of distribution, marketing and advertising."[14]

In many cases filmmakers only go through certain segments of the entire process but still learn from it—there is no failure at Sundance, says Satter—and the emphasis is not on the technical aspects of filmmaking, but on script development, storytelling and working with actors. Among the participants invited each year might be someone who's already established in another field but is at his first experience with film; such as Peter Masterson, the theatre director who developed his first feature film here in 1983, *A Trip to Bountiful* from the Horton Foote play, or James Lapine who did the same thing with *Impromptu* in 1991. Other films that have been produced after being originally developed at the Filmmakers Lab are *The Ballad of Gregorio Cortez* (1982) by Robert Young, the true story of a young Mexican who was chased by a posse in 1901 after killing an American sheriff; *El Norte* (1983) by Gregory Nava about Guatemalans in America; *Promised Land* (1984) by Michael Hoffman; *Once Around* (1987), the first American film by Swedish director Lasse Hallström; *A Dry White Season* (1989) by Euzhan Palcy about apartheid in South Africa; *Johnny Suede* (1992) by Tom Di Cillo with Brad Pitt; *Devil in a Blue Dress* (1995) produced by Denzel Washington and directed by Carl Franklin from the detective novel by Walter Mosley; *Boys Don't Cry* (1999) by Kimberly Peirce about a young woman who wants to be a man; *Me and You and Everyone We Know* (2005), an autobiographical study by video-artist Miranda July; *Half-Nelson* with Ryan Gosling and *A Guide to Recognizing Your Saints*, presented at the festival in 2006.

The people Sundance wants to help are those who have fresh and original ideas, while promoting diversity, regional filmmaking, gay and lesbian points of view, projects by women and ethnic minorities, such as blacks and particularly Indians. One of these filmmakers, Randy Redroad, a Cherokee Indian who developed his project *Cowboys and Indians* (1994) at the Labs, said of films like *Dances with Wolves* and *Thunderheart*, "There's never going to be a Native American perspective until the Native American is behind the camera." Redford is particularly anxious to favor films from a Native American point of view, because he understands the different visual and spiritual sensibility of this people. "I do a lot of collecting of American Indian art. I'm waiting for Indians to enter film. Indian words are not a big part of Indian customs and traditions. They use mostly symbols, chants and dances. I think film can work beautifully for Indians because it's a visual language. We have a division at Sundance where we try to develop Indian filmmaking."[15] He further explains his reasons for including a variety of points of views at Sundance: "I always appreciated the role of diversity, because the American culture is founded on that; it is what keeps this society alive and competitive."[16]

From my personal observation the most unique aspect of Sundance is the friendly atmosphere, the feeling of a small village community where young filmmakers, actors, crew members, staff and experienced industry people—including of course the ubiquitous presence of "Ordinary Bob"—live and eat together. People talk to each other, not only at meetings but informally, in the bar and restaurants; films are screened and discussed every night, scenes are shot on nearby locations on the Sundance property, and participants even bring their children, just like they would for a summer vacation. Redford's reputation and his personal contacts in the industry bring in famous writers, actors and directors as creative advisors, who are available to the student filmmakers as resources; not as teachers who impart theoretical knowledge, but as sounding boards for specific problems. The list of people who have enjoyed coming to Redford's retreat in this capacity is endless: from Sydney Pollack to Arthur Penn, from Jim Brooks to Richard LaGravenese, from Morgan Freeman to Sigourney Weaver. It is probably because, like Redford, they feel an obligation to "put something back into the industry that I felt had been fairly good to me,"[17] but also because they find the exchange of ideas with the newer generation of filmmakers a stimulating two-way street. Pollack says: "I wish there'd been something like Sundance when I was coming along. As it is Sundance helps me anyway. I'm forced to articulate things I take for granted."[18] Many established filmmakers like Sundance because they discover here on the mountains a sense of community that they are missing in the film industry of Los Angeles or New York.

Redford had always missed "a sense of community, of a workplace where you could experiment, exchange ideas and get excited, without some meter ticking away."[19] He loved the energy and creative spirit of independent filmmaking and he had been developing his own films from early on, having set up his production company, Wildwood Enterprises, in 1968; but his intention was not to have a studio, like Francis Ford Coppola did with Zoetrope. He viewed Sundance as something more akin to what George Lucas did with Skywalker Ranch, named after Luke Skywalker, hero of the *Star Wars* saga. "George Lucas is doing something similar at his ranch in California. He's doing pretty much what I am, in the sense that he's giving the land to the development of certain skills for filmmakers. He's creating the environment to develop some aspects of filmmaking. In his case, it's providing the ability to come work on a craft. Ours is much more directed towards script and story and performing, because we really don't have the facilities here. I don't want to get into a lot of buildings and a lot of timber, steel and concrete. I like open space and I think that art does not need a lot to thrive. Based on that, we're going to create a situation that's pretty humble."[20]

Later on, when the Sundance model proved to be working, Redford decided to export it to other countries, turning not only the labs but the festival into an international event. "Once the Lab at Sundance, which is a five week program, became successful and it was refined to a point of becoming portable, then we could move it. We began to go to other countries outside the US and work with film organizations or film programs to take the process of Sundance to them. In exchange we would help them develop their stories, their films in their countries, and then we would bring those films back and show them at Sundance, because they couldn't be seen anywhere else. That has developed and now we have programs in Romania, in Budapest, in Prague, we have Labs in Vietnam, in South Africa and in South America, in Brazil, Buenos Aires, Montevideo, in Guadalajara, Mexico. So basically Sundance has become an international venture where everything is brought to this place in the mountains in Utah, and that is continuing to develop, which gives me a lot of pleasure, because I think the American filmmakers can learn a lot from international filmmakers."[21] Redford had been sensitized about the importance of different world cultures as a young artist living in Europe in the 1950s: "I feel that my life began to happen for me, that I really began to grow, when I went to Europe to study art when I was eighteen. That was a milestone for me. I have a very strong feeling about understanding other cultures, that's one of the reasons why Sundance is there; it's really a cultural exchange as much as an artistic exchange."[22]

While the Sundance workshops continue to take place in the idyllic mountain setting controlled by Redford's minimalist good taste (the Institute celebrated its 25th anniversary in November 2006), the Sundance Film Festival has been expanding out of control, crowded and disorganized, in the sprawling ski resort of Park City, where the hotels are tasteless, the restaurants pricey and transportation a nightmare. The once tranquil atmosphere, that resembled a winter skiing vacation accompanied by a few parties and some night-time screenings, has become a frenzy of industry types with cellular phones fighting to spot the latest discoveries before anyone else. There are no seats to be found in the inadequate screening facilities and invitations to exclusive parties have changed the egalitarian nature of an event, where filmmakers and public could exchange ideas. Redford has acknowledged the problem: "The only thing that attracts Hollywood is success, and when success started to come around the edges at Sundance, Hollywood came to us. Once that onslaught started, I felt we needed to be very careful about staying true to our purpose."[23] In 2006 the situation reached a low point, when the town was full of "luxury lounges" where even minor celebrities were lavished with gifts by companies trying to promote their products; this practice will hopefully be discontinued, since the IRS decreed that the expensive gifts given to presenters at the Oscars have to be declared as income. Festival director Geoffrey Gilmore is openly contemptuous of this practice: "It started to look pretty fucking uncool for rich people to be pulling stuff off shelves and walking away with it."[24] Redford agrees: "It's gotten now almost to a breaking point where there's a fever that has taken over the festival that creates an enormous amount of chaos and excitement and tension. The festival that we do is the same one as we did the first year, we program it exactly the same every year, which is for new voices and more experimental films. But once the merchants come, then the celebrities come. Once they come, the paparazzi come. Once they come, fashion comes. So suddenly you've got a party and all the attention goes there."[25]

Ever since the success of *Sex Lies and Videotape* (1989) directed by Steven Soderbergh and *Reservoir Dogs* (1992) by Quentin Tarantino, there's been an increasing pressure on distributors to acquire the next discovery. The trend was confirmed in 2006 with the commercial and critical success of *Little Miss Sunshine*, a small $8 million budget film that was purchased at Sundance by Fox Searchlight for $10.5 million. Redford regrets the implication: "As happy as I am when a deal is made for a filmmaker, that would make me sad if the festival finally got to that place where it was purely judged by its commercial viability."[26] Sydney Pollack, one of the original founders of the Sundance Institute, also expresses concern that too much success might spoil the original intent of offering an alternative to Hollywood-style films. "This thing has become enormously successful; as a matter of fact its success is its own worst enemy. You have to keep the Institute what it was originally intended; as soon as it starts to get real successful the reasons for it change, it starts to become an entree to the world that this trying to be an alternative to. This is what Bob has had to work very hard to keep from happening, and this is what the pressure is; because once you say, 'Well, if you go to the Institute, that's going to help you get your film produced by a studio,' it starts to be a little bit of a vicious circle. It's good that it's successful, but one has to be vigilant all the time that it doesn't become similar to what it's supposed to be an alternative to."[27]

At one point Redford even claimed to be willing to abandon the Sundance Film Festival, if it got too big and lost its original focus: "I'd rather close it, quite frankly, and let someone else start a festival."[28] That is why he prepared an alternative exhibition venue for independent films and documentaries with the creation of the Sundance Cable Channel in 1996, which is now partnered with NBC Universal and Showtime Networks and is reaching 23,000 subscribers. "I wouldn't have taken on this idea of the cable channel if I hadn't seen curious things happen in Park City. Basically it's just an extension of the original commitment to support the filmmakers, the kind of new ideas and diversity that's best kept alive in independent films. TV may be more mainstream in nature, but it's the best place available to the alternative producer. That's why we're going into cable: to extend the opportunity for filmmakers to take their product to a wider audience."[29]

Another project, the Sundance Cinema Centers, had been developed in 1998, says Redford, to recreate the experience he had as a child going to the Saturday matinees with their varied programs of film serials and cartoons. "For two-and-a-half hours you went into a dark place where you saw a film and many varied forms of shows, and it was really interesting and provocative. That slowly disappeared as business, the profit mentality, has so taken over the industry; that's all gone, in favor of getting as many screening in as possible a day. So the idea is to have these cinema centers be places where you can go in and have an experience of film as culture . . . where people can interact and debate and have a place to view films that would be multi-varied, from experimental films to documentaries to animation to regular features."[30] This plan, which had to be abandoned when General Cinema went bankrupt, has recently been resurrected in a new format: the Sundance Institute Art House Project. An initial group of 14 cinemas nationwide, such as the Kabuki in San Francisco, will feature Sundance films; in May 2006 a pilot program was presented at the Brooklyn Academy of Music in New York.

Other initiatives show that Redford is keeping up with the times and employing the latest technologies to disseminate information. In November 2006 the Sundance Film Festival commissioned six independent filmmakers to create short films for mobile distribution. Redford explains: "Cell phones are fast becoming the 'fourth screen' medium, after television, cinema and computers. We feel this experiment embodies fully our quarter-century dedication to exploring new platforms to support wider distribution of independent voices in filmmaking."[31] In January 2007 the Sundance Channel partnered with YouTube to post daily videos of filmmakers interviews from the festival, with iTunes to sell short documentaries online, and even created a virtual environment on Second Life allowing visitors to attend festival screenings and parties.

Despite the problems with excessive commercialization, Redford is determined to keep the Sundance Film festival focused on its original intention of discovering new filmmakers (a button saying "Focus on Film" was distributed at the 2007 festival). "We program for a mixture of films dealing with race, prejudice, sexuality. It has a uniqueness of vision, as a result it turned out to be a very commercial place," which he finds "kind of ironic."[32] Gilmore says that there are already other festivals featuring established directors, Berlin, Cannes, Venice and Toronto, so their agenda remains the same: "To be responsive to the diversity of American independent film."[33] One thing is clear, this yearly event is very important to Redford and takes up a lot of his time and energy. "It would be nice, just for my ego, for people to know how hard I work on it. I spend a lot of time preparing for it every year, and we always have a post-mortem afterwards, taking a hard look at what went wrong, or what could have been better. Refining it."[34]

With his Sundance venture Redford has put into practice his love for the American West by living and working in a place that he has built in the mountain wilderness. The conflict between farmers in touch with the land and greedy real-estate developers would be the subject of Redford's second film as a director, *The Milagro Beanfield War* (1988), and give him a chance to express his feelings about the constant dichotomy between preservation and development, an issue that he had to face in creating Sundance.

8. THE MILAGRO BEANFIELD WAR

Farmers versus developers

After making his directing debut with *Ordinary People* (1980), Redford decided to base his second film as a director, *The Milagro Beanfield War* (1988), on the cult novel by John Nichols published in 1974. But by the time he became interested in 1979—he was considering making this story his first film as a director—the film rights to the book were owned by Moctezuma Esparza, a respected Chicano producer of Latino-themed TV programs and documentaries who refused to sell out. "Because of his stake in the whole Chicano issue," Redford said, "he didn't just want to give it up." So the two filmmakers decided to work together. "I would have made it anyway. When I get determined about something, I stick to it. But Moctie's involvement, I think, lent a lot of credibility to it."[1] Esparza was impressed by Redford's talent as a director and realized that the involvement of such a prominent Hollywood player could only draw attention to the project: "I considered that stature critical in terms of my goals of changing stereotypes in the general consciousness of the country."[2]

Redford wanted to explore the indigenous Hispanic-Mexican-Indian culture of New Mexico, which is in danger of becoming extinct, in this fable about the struggle of poor farmers to maintain their traditional way of life against the commercial interests of real estate developers. "To me, it's not a book about class struggle. It's bigger than that. It's a piece of history played out against a problem that's endemic to any culture, the threat of extinction.

When you put dollars in contest with tradition it's a pretty tough battle, and in this day and age, tradition seems to be losing."[3]

For Redford this project was a logical extension of his long-standing interest in the preservation of the land and ancient cultures of the American Southwest: "I had already been taken by that culture because I spent time in New Mexico, I have land there, and I understand the triangle in that culture of Anglo, Spanish and Indian."[4] He had developed a familiarity with the Latino way of life as a child, growing up in a poor Mexican neighborhood in Santa Monica: "I grew up in a Latino community, very poor, during the Second World War. We were one of the few Anglo families. So I was very connected to that culture."[5]

He also wanted to try his hand at something lighter than *Ordinary People*, by making an ensemble piece set outdoors in the beauty of the western landscape; therefore he emphasized the humorous and mystical aspects of the novel, with a cinematic style that translated visually the magical realism of Latin American novels, such as *One Hundred Years of Solitude* by Gabriel García Márquez. It is not a coincidence that Redford sponsored Márquez' visit to the United States in 1987, which had been opposed by authorities because the Columbian writer was the director of Cuba's Foundation for Latin American Cinema. In return Márquez invited Redford and other filmmakers to Cuba in 1988 to meet Fidel Castro and visit the Foundation. Redford would then star in *Havana* (1990) directed by Sydney Pollack, a love story about a gambler caught up in the Cuban revolution of 1959, and later produce *The Motorcycle Diaries* (2004), a film about the young Ernesto Che Guevara directed by Walter Salles. He cites these reasons for his interest in that project: "It was about this 23-year-old kid who wants to . . . go on an adventure with his friend. He's naive, he's innocent, he's semi-privileged, hasn't been out of Buenos Aires. Through this trip, he connects with the people, the land, and their health, because he's a doctor."[6] Redford presented in the U.S. the films of Cuban filmmaker Tomás Gutiérrez Alea, *Strawberry and Chocolate* (1994) and *Guantanamera* (1995); and cultural exchanges with Latin America continue to be a major part of the Sundance Institute and Festival programs.

John Nichols, the author of *The Milagro Beanfield War*, was asked to turn his 630-page novel into a screenplay, but the first few drafts failed to produce a shooting script, and it wasn't until the involvement of David Ward, the screenwriter of *The Sting*, that the script was finished and ready to be filmed in 1986. The casting included as many Latino actors as possible; young New York stage actor Chick Vennera was chosen for the lead, Joe Mondragon, although his roots are more Italian-American than Hispanic; the Puertorican Julie Carmen played his wife; 74-year-old Mexican actor Carlos Riquelme was the old Amarante, and Roberto Carricart was the ghost of Mandragon's father, Coyote Angel; Brazilian actress Sonia Braga played the activist Ruby, and Panamanian singer Ruben Blades was the sympathetic sheriff Montoya. On the side of the bad guys are a magnificent Christopher Walken as Montana, the unscrupulous and lethally evil government agent, Richard Bradford as the befuddled developer Ladd Devine, Melanie Griffith as his vapid wife. The good Anglo outsiders who help the locals are Daniel Stern as Herbie Plaat, a sociologist researching his thesis on the native cultures of the Southwest, and John Heard as Charlie Bloom, a retired civil rights lawyer who publishes a local paper and represents the point of view of the author of the novel. John Nichols is a leftist writer of novels like *The Sterile Cuckoo* and *The Wizard of Loneliness*, who moved to Taos, New Mexico in the late 1960s angered by the Vietnam War, and began writing for a local alternative newspaper, *New Mexico Review*. His investigative pieces about land and water conflicts between rural mountain residents and developers provided the raw material for *The Milagro Beanfield War*.

Redford says of the writer: "Nichols was easy to work with. He doesn't smack of ambition, doesn't get uptight about public acceptance of his work. He's a true outlaw, doesn't give a damn about the money." He compares him to another of his favorite writers, Thomas McGuane: "McGuane isn't a Westerner, he's from Michigan, but I think he's onto something—that the true sensibility of the West is the sensibility of the outlaw." Both writers espouse a philosophy that Redford feels akin to, "I feel something congenial about the outlaw, you know, live as you like. Okay, obviously I don't feel as outlaw as I used to, but in the Hollywood establishment, you're always up against something—agents, studio heads, people for whom money is an end, people who are anti-art."[7]

Shooting of *The Milagro Beanfield War* started in August 1986 in Truchas, high on the Sangre de Cristo Mountains not far from Santa Fe. It was very important for Redford to show on film the unspoiled beauty of the land that was to be destroyed by the building of condominiums and golf courses: "The surroundings here lend so much to it. The light is so amazing. There's something so unique about the light, the air, the landscape. The land is another character of the piece."[8] He believes, like the Indians, that the spirit of the earth lives in nature, and that the artist has access to it: "The air and the sky have a mystical quality themselves. Georgia O'Keefe spent a lifetime trying to capture it in her paintings."[9] Once a painter in his youth, Redford cherished the opportunity to express his visual sense in the film medium, by displaying the ineffable beauty of nature in *Milagro* and later in *A River Runs Through it* (1992) and *The Horse Whisperer* (1998).

The film starts with a red sunset and continues with a moonlit night, where a dancing figure in a sombrero prances around playing his harmonica; this musical motif resembles the music Nino Rota wrote for Fellini's *Amarcord*, and this silhouetted figure returns at various moments as an underlying magical thread that will eventually culminate in the triumphant fiesta at the end. Coyote Angel is a ghost who knows the future and he comes around to chat and give friendly advice to Amarante, the oldest inhabitant of the village, who worships his altar of wooden statues and remembers all the ancient superstitions (such as not to sleep with your bed pointing West if you want to avoid stomach troubles). The East Coast sociologist will later explain to the uneducated old man how the missionaries, who arrived with the Spanish Conquistadores, replaced the pagan gods of the Indians with Catholic saints, and that the villagers still practice idolatry by praying to statues of saints.

Ruby, a local woman who works as an auto mechanic and a plumber, is very aware that her people's way of life is in danger of disappearing, that the young are moving elsewhere to find work and that her hometown will end up as a village of old people; she knows that the planned resort development called Miracle Valley, the English word for their village of Milagro, will make it impossible for the locals to survive in a changed economy of higher taxes. She convinces the big city lawyer Bloom, the defender of lost causes, to come to a town meeting to explain this inevitable development, but the ignorant villagers are divided by petty infighting. The catalyzing impetus for her fight is mercifully provided by Joe Mandragon's inconsiderate act of letting the water from an irrigation canal spill onto his father's field and growing beans on it. This had been done for generations, before an incomprehensible government law had forbidden the locals from using the water, in order to covertly favor the real-estate developers, who could then force the farmers to sell the land when their fields dried up.

Ruby smiles when she drives her red pick-up to see the water flow on the ground and says, "I knew José Mondragon couldn't go through his entire life without attempting at least one great thing." This act of defiance slowly but surely focuses the widespread discontent and convinces the community to fight for their rights; eventually Mondragon, who has shot Amarante by mistake, is chased by a posse led by a local sheriff sympathetic to his cause. In a scenario that resembles the chase of the Indian in *Tell Them Willie Boy is Here*, the ineffectual posse returns home at the end of the day, and the evil secret agent, hired by the governor to protect the interests of the developers, follows the hero as he climbs over rocky cliffs and loses his rifle under the pursuer's gunfire. It's the intervention of another sympathetic villager, Horsethief Shorty, that saves his life. The people claim victory when the governor calls off his henchman, who's about to arrest Mondragon as a fugitive from justice accused of attempted murder. Just like in the case of Sonny Steele and the AMPCO Corporation in *The Electric Horseman*, it had become politically dangerous for the authorities to ignore the swelling of popular support that the rebellious hero had caused. The triumphant conclusion is that the community has been able to come together, if only for a short but wonderful moment, as they all dance and sing in Spanish during a spontaneous fiesta to celebrate the harvest of the beanfield. His picture, says Redford, is "about a battle being won, even if the war is being lost, a little battle to preserve a culture for a time."[10]

This is how the director explains his intentions in the telling of this fable: "That history is fascinating and the remnants of that original history, about the intermarriage of the Spanish and the Indian, is what is left in some of these remote villages in the mountains of Northern New Mexico. Those people believe what they believe, they are the way they are, they're quirky, they're unpredictable; they're in a land that is so powerful and magical, there is no way you can control it. You pit that against not only the Anglo culture but the Anglo sensibility, you're going to have a clash, and you have for me a wonderfully dramatic situation. John Nichols decided to make it almost like a fairy tale, which I thought was wonderful. I was enchanted by it and I wanted to deliver something that I also felt that I understood, which is that this is real for these people, they do believe in ghosts, they believe that people deceased come back and talk to them and bother them. And there's something about our culture that is so rooted in reality that we find it hard to accept those things. I thought it was wonderful to explore that."[11]

The Milagro Beanfield War is clearly not a Western, but it is set in the West and it deals with the dilemma of development versus conservation; in this case it is not the unspoiled wilderness that needs to be preserved, but the traditional way of life of small farming communities. This is why Redford was interested in the story: "I am an environmentalist, I have for a long time believed in the power of the land and the need to preserve a lot of it from the onslaught of development; so this had at the crux the tension between the old traditional people who were totally impoverished, but had control of a small patch of land that had water, and the water belonged to one character who is living hand-to-mouth. Against that, all surrounding it, this massive development with golf courses, this big robber-baron developer that wants to take everything, wants to take that land, but mostly the water that comes with it so they can water their golf course. And through one single little tiny move that this one character makes, out of sheer defiance—he's just stubborn—it cracks open a crack that just spreads all over the whole place and becomes an out-and-out war."[12]

The fight between evil developers and government authorities—who employ a secret agent whose methods are decidedly outside of legal propriety, just like certain western outlaws—can be compared to the struggles between big ranchers and small farmers during the Johnson Country War of 1892, which has been the subject of many Westerns, from *The Westerner* (1940) with Gary Cooper directed by William Wyler to *Shane* (1952) by George Stevens, from *Heaven's Gate* (1982) directed by Michael Cimino to *Pale Rider* (1985) by Clint Eastwood.

Another interesting aspect of *The Milagro Beanfield War* is that it serves as a demonstration that Redford has given women important roles in the films that he directed. In this film the young farmer commits his act of defiance almost unconsciously, and it is his wife who complains for not having been consulted about such an important decision that will affect the future of the family. And the real soul of the story is Ruby, she's the one person who understands completely the political meaning of the villagers' defiance; not intellectually, but because she has a visceral connection to her people and their traditions. The intellectuals are somewhat more ineffectual. Some fun is made of the lawyer who has secret sexual encounters with local women, raising Ruby's curiosity; it's an amusing jab at the womanizing behavior that is typical of many men, even the politically committed kind.

In the third film he directed, *A River Runs Through It*, Redford enlarged considerably the role of Norman's fiancé, Jessie; and in *Quiz Show* it's the wives, Goodwin's and Stempel's, who are making their husbands reflect on their morally questionable behavior. Even in *Ordinary People*, where the mother is responsible for her son's emotional problems, the woman has a central role. In *The Legend of Bagger Vance*, it's the protagonist's former fiancé who helps him regain his self-confidence. In *The Horse Whisperer*, even though much fun is made of the nervous behavior of the career woman from the East, the western man admires her determination and ends up falling in love with her.

If we examine the female protagonists of Redford's Westerns, we find that women are not treated as objects of obscene lust, as in *The Wild Bunch* for instance, but in a much more respectful way, even though they are still portrayed from a male perspective.

Elizabeth, the director of the Indian Reservation in *Tell Them Willie Boy is Here*, represents the civilizing influence of an educated woman from the East who questions the necessity of violence in the West; a tradition that started with Molly, the schoolteacher from *The Virginian*, the 1902 novel by Owen Wister that was made into the 1929 Western classic with Gary Cooper directed by Victor Fleming. Eventually the western hero reaffirms the necessity of violence as the new law on the frontier, but in the end he finds that his actions have been unfair, according to his own code of honor. Etta Place in *Butch Cassidy and the Sundance Kid* is also a schoolteacher with a distaste for violence, particularly when it means seeing the men she loves doomed to death by the inner logic of violence in the Wild West. In *Jeremiah Johnson* the woman who helps the mountain man is an Indian, and this, according to New Western historians, had been a tradition in the settling of the West. "Women historians have shown how the first white fur trappers and traders relied on Indian wives both as laborers and essential liaisons in their first contact with Native American societies."[13] This idea is presented in more recent Westerns, like *Dances with Wolves*, where Stands with Fists is a white woman raised by Indians who serves as mediator for the white man to understand Indian culture.

As an aside, it's interesting to see how in the 1990s the myth of Pocahontas was re-proposed by Disney in a politically correct cartoon version, which proves that the new interpretations of Western history have trickled down into popular culture. The significance of the young Indian princess who helps the colonists, based on plays written between 1805 and 1855, used to be that the sexualized woman who represented the land recognized the superiority of the white man by falling in love with John Smith; while in the animated *Pocahontas* (1994) a distinction is made between the good white man and the evil commander, whose only interest is to rape the resources of the New World. Russell Means, the former AIM leader who recorded the voice of Pocahontas' father, commends the Disney version for exposing "the truth about why European men came over here in the first place. They came to rob, rape, pillage the land and kill Indians. That's the Columbian legacy." He also explains the special significance of the woman in Indian society: "The movie introduces the Indian people to the children through the woman, rightly and justly so. Because the vast majority of Indian people are matriarchal societies. The women are our strength and power. Pocahontas proves out to be wiser than the wise man, wiser than her father, and tells the children that bone structure and pigmentation are not important in human relationships. That is a message kids will see over and over for years."[14]

The most fully realized portrait of the beauty and innocence of the famous Indian princess and her influence on Captain Smith, who is tempted to abandon his duties to run away with her, is to be found in Terrence Malick's magical film, *The New World* (2005).

With Redford, we can see that he's aware of women's strength and their moral influence on men, of their traditional place in the American West, as expressed by Robert Warshow: "In the American mind, refinement, virtue, civilization, Christianity itself, are seen as feminine, and therefore women are often portrayed as possessing some kind of deeper wisdom, while the men, for all their apparent self-assurance, are fundamentally childish."[15] As we noticed, the portrayal of women in *Butch Cassidy and the Sundance Kid* and *Jeremiah Johnson* reveals a male bias; but that's understandable and somewhat inevitable for that time. Sandra Schackel says: "Since men have written and directed Western films almost exclusively, women's roles tend to reflect a male perspective," and this "dominates the genre in ways in which women's roles are played out in accordance with male expectations of female behavior," therefore they "are imbued with traits traditionally considered feminine: passivity, dependence, gentleness, and sensitivity."[16]

In Redford's later films, particularly the ones that he directed, the women characters are given more weight; even though the central conflict of the stories—in *Ordinary People*, *A River Runs Through It* and *Quiz Show*—is about men who have a problem in conforming to their fathers' ideals.

However, Redford continued to play male characters with a superior attitude towards the women they eventually fall in love with. In *Up Close and Personal* (1996) the TV anchorwoman played by Michelle Pfeiffer starts off as ignorant, stupid and clumsy, before learning to be a professional under the guidance of an older male mentor. In a similar way the professionalism of the TV reporter played by Jane Fonda in *The Electric Horseman* is visually undermined by her high heels and tight jeans; she modifies her careless behavior when she understands the moral superiority of the cowboy's quest to free the horse. This theme is echoed once again in *The Horse Whisperer*, when a humorous comment about the woman's white hat underlines the inappropriateness of her urban attire in a western setting; in the end the male sacrifices his own desire for love to adhere to a higher moral standard that does not condone infidelity in a marriage. This dismissive attitude towards women is revealing of Redford's own male bias, his predilection towards portraying serious and self-assured men, bemused but at the same time intrigued by women's vanity and frivolities; his characters invariably end up falling in love with these women despite their flaws, but then leaving them in one way or another.

9. A RIVER RUNS THROUGH IT

Fly-fishing in harmony with nature

Robert Redford chose *A River Runs Through It* (1992) as his third project as director, because he considered it an appropriate vehicle to tell a story about the American West, at a time—the 1920s—when a way of living close to nature still informed the country's unique character and values. "There were enough elements that merged together to make this piece something I really wanted to do. It dealt with the environment, in a time and place that I believe was very special, because it helped form a way of life that embodies the strength of our country. This film represents a period of American history in our beginning, the end of a time when things were done by horse and by hand, before machines took over, before radio and television. It was unquestionably a different lifestyle, and yet it was then that the image of the West, that's supposedly the backbone of our strength, was formed."[1]

In Norman Maclean's autobiographical novella the sport of fly-fishing, the state of grace one can achieve while catching the silvery trout that swim in the mountain rivers, is equated with being connected with God and the sacredness of nature. The narration over the opening sentence says: "In our family there was no clear line between religion and fly-fishing." Redford believes in this idea as well, "When you're fly-fishing—and you really have to do it in order to know exactly what it is—there's something very powerful and deep about the experience, particularly when you do it well, some real communion with nature that goes on, that's totally peaceful and really ancient."[2] In the film as in the book, the physical and spiritual grace necessary to fish well is compared with the creative work of an artist.

The author's stern father, a Presbyterian minister, had instructed his two boys in the discipline of fly-fishing from an early age, and the younger brother Paul was able to transcend his teachings and turn the sport into an art form. It is implied, of course, that the older brother Norman is also creating a work of art by writing about his life in this book. At one point the writer-narrator comments, while watching his younger brother fishing: "I then saw something remarkable. For the first time Paul broke free of our father's instructions into a rhythm all of his own. He called it 'shadow-casting' and I realized that my brother, in the time I was away, had become an artist. At that moment I knew, surely and clearly, that I was witnessing perfection. My brother stood before us, not on a bank of the Blackfoot River, but suspended above the earth, free from all its laws, like a work of art. And I knew, just as surely and clearly, that life is not a work of art and that moment could not last." Stylistically Redford used the voice of the narrator—which he recorded himself—to maintain the beauty of Maclean's language.

Maclean, a professor of English literature at the University of Chicago, had written *A River Runs Through It* (1976) when he was already in his seventies, as a way to come to terms with the tragic death of his younger brother, who on the surface was a golden boy blessed with a natural ease in his relationships with people and with nature, but underneath had self-destructive tendencies that manifested themselves in a love for drink, gambling and women; and eventually caused his demise. Redford says he cast Brad Pitt, who looks a lot like he did when he was younger, not because of their "cosmetic" similarities, but because he identified with the character's duality. "It's true, were I younger, I probably would have wanted to play that part; but it really had more to do with what was inside the character, someone who on the outside looked very healthy and all-American but inside carried a dark side, there was a dark shadow underneath."[3] Pitt explains Paul's inner dilemma: "Paul has grown up in a Christian family, with a certain religion and a way of life, and he was told that this is the way it should be, but he's caught in a bind, because he has other beliefs that he can't share with his family. His problem was that he had grown up with certain family values, that were put upon him without options and pointed him in one direction, but then there were other things, that he didn't quite understand, that started pulling him in another direction; so he was caught in the middle between the two. He found himself having desires and beliefs that didn't fall within his family's plans or the way he was raised. When Paul comes home, he's a different person than when he's out, because out there he was freer; so he was living two lives, which didn't hook up because it was not spoken—communication was not a big thing in his family, you were supposed to be a man and respect other people's manhood—so there was always this conflict and this dilemma, that caused guilt and pretense. In my opinion, if you're not allowed to be yourself, if an acceptance level isn't found and you have to fake it with people who are very important to you, this sooner or later will lead to self-destruction."[4]

This was another reason why Redford was interested in *A River Runs Through It*, because it had a similar family dynamics as *Ordinary People*. "It also dealt with matters of the heart and interpersonal relationships within the family, one of the toughest subjects, because what you talk about and what you don't talk about will affect the nature of the family's development."[5] In both films the inability to express openly emotions and ideas that diverge from the accepted family values causes repressed feelings that result in transgressive behavior or suicidal tendencies.

Redford has an appreciation for this type of old-fashioned upbringing: "The fact that the father raised his sons that way had a lot to do with the ethics of the time and place. The family lived closer to nature than most of us do today, therefore they had to develop very strong physical skills in order to deal with it."[6] He felt in tune with this tale about two brothers raised in Montana in the 1920s because it reminded him of the way he himself was raised in the 1940s: "I was raised in a different time, but my family also comes from a Scots-Irish ethic and believes in the idea of communication more through storytelling than through expressing your emotions or feelings. I was also given a heavy discipline as a kid in order to survive, not as religion but as a way of behaving; it meant being stoic in the face of adversity, not ever complaining, learning things on your own. That was not a time in our society, nor in my family, where people spilled their guts out on the table, like they do now. There was not a lot of therapy and psychoanalysis, there weren't the institutions to buffer you against the forces of nature or society; and in Norman Maclean's time it was even less so, so there were similar characteristics in our upbringing."[7]

While in *Ordinary People* the intervention of the psychiatrist helps the suicidal boy deal with the repressed family issues, in *A River Runs Through It* the act of writing alleviates the guilt the author feels for not having been able to help and understand his brother. In both cases Redford the filmmaker illustrates for the viewer family dilemmas that he has lived himself and merges the personal drama into a larger social issue, the destruction of the natural environment. "*A River Runs Through It* is unquestionably about sadness and loss, it's about the joys and mysteries of life, about that inexplicable part of life that leaves us wondering about what happened. It's about the sadness of what we've lost in this country, as far as the beauty of nature and the land, as far as the way we lived our lives within the family. When you lose a family member or someone you loved, there's a big ghost in your presence for the rest of your life; you ask yourself: Could I have done something to help him?"[8]

As he had done with *Jeremiah Johnson* and *Electric Horseman*, Redford expresses through *A River Runs Through It* his nostalgia for an earlier time, when people lived closer to nature and survived by working with their hands and a few hand-made tools. "When I was a kid the natural environment was just there for you and available, it was not something you had to go find; it was all around you, so you just went into it and did what you had to do. Now, as things get removed from our society and we see the mistakes of the past, we seem to be reaching out to try and find ways to hold on to them."[9] He thinks this is the reason why fly-fishing has become so popular: "I suspect it's in response to what has been taken away from us of a natural order; that's why so many people started fishing that used to go to a gym to work out. We don't do much labor outside anymore and we have to travel distances with special equipment to be in nature, so that's probably a way to try and hold on to something primal."[10]

Redford as a visual director and ardent environmentalist wants to express in moving images what the American West looked like before it became spoiled by the encroaching of development, in order to inspire younger generations to preserve what's left. "I have very strong feelings about what we're doing to the environment in a country that is so blessed in terms of resources; and if you love it as I do, then you take it personally, when you have to sit by and watch these great resources that have such an importance being savaged by mindless people. So for me, since I don't believe in overt political propaganda in films, I thought the best way to get a point across would be to show the American people a reminder of how things were; for younger people who would never know how it was, except through books and photographs, I would show it live and say that this is the way our country used to look all the time. And that may evoke enough interest to have them begin to mind what moves they made; and with the older people it would be a piece of nostalgia asking them to remember those times."[11]

We can also read between the lines a comment about the ancient Indian belief of a spiritual communion between the hunted animals—such as the buffaloes—and the hunter. To Norman his father's teachings implied that the trout would not allow anyone to catch them who didn't deserve it; the line from the book repeated in the film goes: "If our father had had his say, nobody who did not know how to fish would be allowed to disgrace a fish by catching it."

Edward Zwick, who directed *Legends of the Fall* (1994) from the Jim Harrison novella, was onto a similar idea, when he explored Tristan's identification with the bear: "There are tales about men who in battle became bears, or shape shifters; they had this beast within them and when the bear came out they would kill friend and foe alike."[12] Tristan, who is described as a "force of nature," had been raised by an Indian housekeeper (Tantoo Cardinal), and had his father's old Cree scout, One Stab (Gordon Tootoosis), as mentor; he had learned from this Indian storyteller the skills of a warrior and the spiritual beliefs of the Indians. Brad Pitt, who not coincidentally was chosen to play Tristan after making *A River Runs Through It*, explains, "It's always about respect for the land, everything concerned with nature is about respect. It's not that I have power, that I can kill this deer and it makes me stronger. No, it's respect for the deer, for what he represents, and I can learn from him; the deer is providing me to live through him."[13] Zwick talks about the oneness with nature "of a people who lived on the land in touch with their universe," which is something that "had to do with dignity, with the inner fire, the beast inside of them."[14] Unfortunately that "had already been lost by the Native American and then it was lost by the culture that had taken it away from them;"[15] by the white men who settled on the western frontier in the early 1900s, like Tristan's father, who, as a colonel in the Army, had seen the horrors of the Indian wars and the senseless slaughter of innocent Indians.

In Redford's view the respect for animals and the spirituality of nature is something that a young man learns from his elders, like Bear Claw in *Jeremiah Johnson*, and that the white frontiersmen who first explored the American wilderness had learned from the Native Americans who inhabited this land before them. He expressed this idea in his films, in his interest in Indian art and culture through the years and in his political commitment to Native American causes.

Although in *A River Runs Through It* the principal dynamic is between the two brothers and their father, the women characters have been given much more space in the film than in the original book. The two mothers are portrayed as the soul of their families and the emotional anchor for their men, and Jessie (Emily Lloyd), the author's fiancé, is a well-developed character. This is how screenwriter Richard Friedenberg describes her: "You have to remember that the twenties was a great time of liberation for women, it was then that they got the vote. Jessie was a flapper, she drove a car by herself, she drank, she went to college and she did what she pleased. Perhaps it's a misconception that all women of that era were like Zelda Fitzgerald; Jessie was definitely a modern woman, as opposed to her mother, who was still a woman of the 19th century."[16] Emily Lloyd says: "I actually met the daughter of the real person, Jessie, who was Norman Maclean's wife, and she told me some wonderful stories about her mother that I wish we could have seen in the film, but this was predominantly a story about the boys; anyway it helped me to know those things and bring them to the character. In fact in the book there are only two lines describing her, luckily I read the screenplay first, otherwise I don't think I would have accepted to play the part."[17] This is how the actress sees the character of Jessie, who had a different upbringing than Norman's: "The Scots have a very honest quality about them, women especially. In keeping with the Scotch heritage and background women are very strong, they really stand behind their men. So Jessie was strong and very supportive of the men in the family, as it was customary in that time, without being subservient or deferring to the male; at the same time there was a camaraderie between Jess and Norman that continued for the rest of their lives. Jessie's family was Methodist—compared to the Maclean's, who were Presbyterians and had difficulty communicating—so she was more free and there was a good contrast between her and Norman. He wasn't truly able to express his feelings, but when she was sure he was really there for her, they were able to form this incredible bond between them."[18]

Robert Redford justifies his male-oriented tale as consistent with the times: "As tempting as it was, there was very little time to accommodate all the characters, unless we were willing to get distracted from the main issue of the brothers and the relationship with their father; so we were forced to use broad brush strokes and suggest a great deal with short scenes. The mother was hardly developed at all in the book, and Jessie existed in such short shrifts that she had to be invented. While we were doing this, we couldn't help incorporating a bit of the way we feel today about women, after what's happened to their role in society; the fact is that in those times women had to defer their strength to the shadows for the admiration of the men. I wanted to illustrate the strength of the women without distorting the accuracy to the time period, so I had to thread a very fine line."[19]

This proves that Redford is aware of the changed role of women in our time and has tried to incorporate this new sensibility in his work, although a main focus of his films has been the difficult relationship between men and their fathers.

Davis points out that this subject had become a hot topic in the early 1990s, after the publication of Robert Bly's *Iron John: A Book About Men* (1990), where the author claimed that "a whole new approach is needed to restore the idea of masculinity," and offered as a solution ways "to rediscover a process by which boys can be initiated into manhood by their elders, the wise men of the tribe, and thus, gaining a sense of ritual and form, achieve reconciliation with parents, women, and the real strength of their own natures."[20] Traditionally "the question of how to act like a man and indeed of figuring out what a man is supposed to be and do is central to the Western,"[21] and Redford dealt with this subject by filming a book like *A River Runs Through It* by Norman Maclean, which, said Cawelti, "has already become a Western classic of a very different sort than the usual story of regeneration through violence."[22] In his film the teaching of this stern religious father to his sons are of a spiritual nature, about achieving a sense of harmony with all things, like in the flowing of a river.

10. NATIVE AMERICANS

The Dark Wind and Incident at Oglala

A real concern for Native Americans is one of the themes that run through Redford's work, not only in films like *Tell Them Willie Boy Is Here* and *Jeremiah Johnson*, but in his interests as a producer. Redford produced the documentary *Incident at Oglala* (1992), directed by Michael Apted, about Leonard Peltier, the leader of the American Indian Movement jailed for the murder of FBI men; the television film *Grand Avenue* (1996) from the novel by Greg Sarris, about the lives of three Native American families in Santa Rosa, California; the feature film *The Dark Wind* (1990), directed by Errol Morris from the novel by Tony Hillerman about an Indian detective (Lou Diamond Phillips) who uses ancient mystical powers to solve a murder mystery; *The Education of Little Tree* (1997) from the novel by Forrest Carter, directed by Richard Friedenberg, the screenwriter of *A River Runs Through It*. After a pause of several years caused by economic difficulties, Redford continued to produce films from Tony Hillerman's novels about Indian Officer Jim Chee, now played by Adam Beach, and his superior Joe Leaphorn (Wes Studi); only this time they were made for television (PBS): *Skinwalkers* (2002), *Coyote Waits* (2003), *A Thief of Time* (2004).

When Redford bought the film rights to Tony Hillerman's crime novels about Navajo tribal policemen, his intention was to produce a series of low-budget films that explored the Indian cultures of the Southwest, through his North Fork production company (founded in 1988 in partnership with Garth Drabinski, director of the Cineplex-Odeon Canadian theater chain). Redford says that North Fork is dedicated to films "that deal with regional matters indigenous to different cultures."[1] The first novel to be put into production—in association with Carolco Pictures—was *The Dark Wind*, published in 1982, a murder mystery about drug trafficking and witchcraft, narrated from the perspective of the greenhorn Navajo detective investigating the case, Jim Chee. Redford chose as director documentary filmmaker Errol Morris, who had never made a feature film before but had shown his original talent in the acclaimed documentary *The Thin Blue Line* (1988). *The Dark Wind* had a tortured history and was eventually released directly to video in 1993; but Redford, who was still interested in filming other Hillerman mysteries, found alternate financing for them as TV movies. His son, James Redford, wrote the screenplay for the first one, *Skinwalkers*, about the legendary witches that can fly and turn themselves into dogs or wolves and might be murdering shamans. *A Thief of Time* is about the disappearance of a woman anthropologist who was studying the ancient Anasazi culture. *Coyote Waits*, about the murder of a Navajo cop falsely attributed to an old drunken shaman, includes a missing history professor in search of Butch Cassidy.

Redford felt a connection to these thrillers that illuminate various aspects of the Navajo religion, because in the late 1970s he had started to explore the spiritual beliefs of the Native Americans. "I've become interested in the connection between archeology and cosmology. A certain kind of spiritualism that I can't quite define, coming from the cultural roots of the Southwestern Indians. It's the whole idea that there were highly developed societies here, in our country, long before history records them. And how that relates to history and to energy and to spirituality. I've never been a follower of organized religion, although I guess I've been, without knowing it, a spiritual person. I've always been able to get high on natural elements. And the human spirit really does interest me."[2]

The production of *The Dark Wind* first ran into difficulties, because the American Indian Registry for the Performing Arts protested the casting of Lou Diamond Phillips, who claimed to be part Cherokee, as well as Filipino, Scotch-Irish and Spanish; but had failed to produce the required documentation. Phillips had played a Mexican bandit of Navajo descent in the youth Westerns *Young Guns* (1988) and *Young Guns II* (1990) about the adventures of Billy the Kid and his gang, which were written by John Fusco and starred Emilio Estevez, Charlie Sheen, Kiefer Sutherland and Christian Slater. Phillips, who had played a Lakota Sioux in the film *Renegades* (1989), said that the Sioux had made him an honorary member of the tribe for his portrayal of American Indians in films, and given him the Indian name Star Keeper. "I'm Cherokee by blood but I've just been adopted by the Sioux tribe. On Labor Day, I'm going to the Pine Ridge Reservation in South Dakota for my naming ceremony."[3]

Redford and Morris had been looking for a full-blooded Native American for the lead, but had not been able to find anyone with the necessary acting experience, while Phillips had the right look and enough acting talent to carry the film. Fred Ward, also a non-Indian, was cast as Sergeant Jim Chee's superior, Navajo Police Lieutenant Joe Leaphorn; but Gary Farmer, a full-blooded Mohawk, landed the part of Hopi Deputy Sheriff Albert "Cowboy" Dashee. It is through the collaboration between these two policemen from different tribal cultures—one Hopi, the other Navajo—that the mystery is eventually unraveled, and both Hopi and Navajo languages are spoken in the film. Dashee translates Chee's questions into Hopi and gives him access to his people and their mystical beliefs, while Chee can speak Navajo as he questions his people, and his knowledge and respect for tribal traditions allows him to get information, uncover contradictions, and discover that the accusations made by a white man against a Navajo are false.

The production had the cooperation of the Navajo Nation and of the Hopi Tribal Council, while shooting on the Hopi and Navajo Reservations near Tuba City in the Painted Desert of Northern Arizona; however, the Hopi religious leaders of the Shungopavi village were opposed to setting the murderous climate during one of their secret religious ceremonies, which they considered sacrilegious to reveal on film. Caught in the middle of the traditional hostility between Navajos and Hopis, while filming a novel that was perceived as sympathetic to the Navajos, director Morris had trouble obtaining permission to film in several key locations; then the problems were compounded by inclement weather (unseasonable snow delayed the filming). Finally, the bankruptcy of Carolco created distribution problems for the completed film, and it is not the director's cut that appears in the existing video. Nevertheless, *The Dark Wind* stands as an honorable attempt to present the Indians' way of thinking about the world, by entering into the mind of a Navajo investigator who is sensitive to his tribe's "Old Ways."

It is important to notice that, even though the Tony Hillerman series of Navajo-themed mystery novels have been written by a white man, they are often used as textbooks to get Hopi and Navajo children interested in their own culture; therefore they're obviously respectful of the Indian culture and in tune with Redford's own sensibilities.

Tony Hillerman had created the character of Joe Leaphorn for his first novel, *The Blessing Way* (1970); the Navajo tribal policeman has a degree in anthropology and considerable skepticism about his people's spiritual beliefs. The writer says: "Here's a Navajo who's a very intelligent fellow, and he's not going to be a fundamentalist in terms of his religion. He may well be a religious man, but he's going to see mythology in a more abstract, poetic sense."[4] In 1980, for his novel *People of Darkness*, Hillerman created a younger Navajo cop, Jim Chee, an Indian who had grown up with the Wounded Knee generation of Native Americans concerned with rediscovering their traditional culture. The author, who had taught journalism at New Mexico University in Albuquerque in the 1960s, says, "Chee is a composite of 20 years of college students. It was back in that time when the counterculture was flowering and there was a revival of romanticism."[5] The younger, less cynical cop is interested in the "Old Ways" of his people and is studying to be a shaman. And that is what attracted Redford, "Jim Chee interests me as a man who wants to retain his tradition and roots but also has been to college and is a modern man. He's caught between two worlds."[6]

In the film *The Dark Wind* Sergeant Chee relieves the boredom of stakeouts by learning how to chant and perform healing ceremonies. He shows his boss a business card he had printed to offer his services, that reads *The Blessing Way*, the title of Hillerman's first novel. Leaphorn says there might be a contradiction between being a "singer" and a cop; but in the end the mother of Joseph Musket, the falsely accused Navajo who had been murdered by the white magician, asks Chee to purify her son's possessions by chanting. Earlier Chee had become convinced of Musket's innocence, when his mother told him that, after being released from jail, her son had gotten a "sing" to purify his body and mind, which signified a return to the "Old Ways" and a new beginning to erase the mistakes of the past. The conclusion is that Chee is accepted as a shaman by his people, while still remaining a cop. It also falls to him to explain the *Modus operandi* of the Navajo witches, called "Skinwalkers"—the title of another Hillerman novel—and the meaning of the "Dark Wind" of the title, when he tells the murdered pilot's wife that Navajos do not believe in revenge. "Traditionally speaking, Navajos believe that when a man does something wrong or destructive or just plain crazy, it's because of the dark wind that is blowing through him; and it makes no sense to seek revenge. You just stay out of his way until he gets cured and it all blows over."

Hillerman is interested in showing Indian culture the way it is today on the Navajo reservations of the Southwest, not in idealizing their lost native lifestyles of two-hundred-years ago; that's why he portrays Indians as full human beings, good cops as well as criminal characters. He's very impressed with their ancient religious beliefs, their deep family loyalty, their attachment to the clan, their disregard of material possessions; he particularly appreciates their ability to live in harmony with their surroundings and to feel the beauty of nature: "I find it remarkable how many Navajos will talk frankly and almost emotionally about the beauty around them."[7] Redford shares the author's admiration for the Indian cultures of the Southwest, and is interested in the issues that affect that society today, like the conflict over water rights between Hopis and Navajos, caused by arbitrary decisions of the federal government, which is the background of *The Dark Wind* and other Hillerman novels. Redford had explored a similar theme in *The Milagro Beanfield War*.

At the time that *The Dark Wind* went into production in 1990, the success of Kevin Costner's *Dances with Wolves* had started a trend in Hollywood of politically correct Westerns informed by a new sensibility toward the plight of the Indians and the genocide they had been subjected to at the hands of the American government. Film critics like Michael Wilmington pointed out that there had been many other pro-Indian films in Hollywood history, from *The Vanishing American* (1925) and *Broken Arrow* (1950) to *Cheyenne Autumn* (1964) and *Little Big Man* (1970). A welcome change was that Costner's film employed real Indian actors like Graham Greene and Tantoo Cardinal, the Sioux were speaking their ancient Lakota language, and the historical accuracy of their costumes and traditions was researched and respected.

But *Dances with Wolves* was an emotional and nostalgic homage to the joyous tribal life of the Plains Indians before the arrival of the white man, and it perpetuated the myth of the "noble savage," which dates back to James Fenimore Cooper's *Leatherstocking Tales*, and can be as damaging as the stereotype of the drunken Indian.

Michael Mann, who filmed *The Last of the Mohicans* (1992) as a sweepingly romantic love story, said that his research into the period proved that in the American colonies of the 18th century the Indians and the white settlers were in daily contact in complex and very human ways, that the Indians had "as much intelligence, aggression, libido, humor and cynicism as we might have today," and that Fenimore Cooper was "guilty of appropriating their history" when he "robbed them of their accomplishments" by reducing them to "noble savages."[8] Mann chose Russell Means, the leader of the American Indian movement, who organized the protest at Wounded Knee with Dennis Bank in 1973, to play Chingachgook as a chief who sees the historical inevitability of the demise of his people. In this way the politically aware Mann was making the connection to the present.

Bruce Beresford, who directed *Black Robe* (1991) about French Jesuits converting Indians in Quebec in the 17th century, said that in his film "the Indians, although they're treated with respect, are not really shown as noble savages, which is a pretty comical interpretation. I've tried very hard to show them the way I think they were really living, which was rough."[9] In *Black Robe* a distinction is made among the various tribes of Indians living on the East Coast of North America: the friendly Algonquin, the fierce Iroquois, the Christianized Hurons. They are the same tribes described by Mann in *The Last of the Mohicans*: the Hurons, the Iroquois, the Mohicans (which were part of the Algonquin tribe), and the Mohawks. Mann says that these Indians of the North East had already been dealing and trading with Europeans for 150 years by 1757 and that the various groups coexisted peacefully on the basis of their common task, which was survival on the frontier, in tough times on a dangerous and inhospitable land. These Indians were not the same as the Plains Indians of traditional Westerns, such as the Sioux, the Cheyennes or the Comanches; Beresford says, "I'd always thought in terms of Indians like from American Westerns, charging across the plains on horses. It wasn't like that at all. These were woodland Indians; they were farmers and they lived in big villages."[10] The point of the film is to show that the intention of the Jesuits—in Quebec like in Central and South America—was to protect the Indians; but inadvertently they destroyed them. Their intervention had disastrous results that they never foresaw: once converted to Christianity, the Hurons dropped their defenses and were wiped out by the Iroquois.

Armando Prats in *Invisible Natives* observes that in classic Westerns, rather than a historical figure whose culture keeps changing, the Indian is represented as a fixed image that belongs to the past: "The Indian ceases to have a history, or at least a story worth telling, following the triumph of western civilization." Even in revisionist films such as *Dances with Wolves* (1990), *Last of the Mohicans* (1992), *Geronimo: An American Legend* (1994), that strive for historical accuracy, "to follow the lives of these Indians is to document in poignant detail the tragic . . . march of the native people toward cultural extinction."[11]

British director Michael Apted felt that Costner's film *Dances with Wolves* was like "historical exorcism, a rather romantic Hollywood way for the American people to remove their guilt about the whole American Indian issue," and he wanted to show that the problem was not over, that the issues were still very much the same in the Indian reservations today; when he was given the "unusual opportunity to do the same thing through two eyes, that of the documentarian and the fiction filmmaker."[12] Apted was asked by Robert Redford to direct the documentary *Incident at Oglala* about Leonard Peltier, and he was also chosen by producer Robert De Niro to direct John Fusco's script *Thunderheart* (1992), about the covert activities of the FBI in the Pine Ridge Oglala Sioux Reservation of South Dakota.

Redford said he felt an obligation to deal with this issue, because "these people were not only impoverished, but threatened with extinction as a culture and as individuals."[13] Apted agreed with Redford that it was "extremely sad that an indigenous population should be treated this way,"[14] and sympathized with the battle that was fought by the American Indian Movement in the 1970's to protect their human, cultural and religious rights and not give up their heritage in order to assimilate into mainstream American culture. He thought it was important to show that "these people still have vitality, a lot of dignity and pride in their culture, although their impoverishment is almost beyond belief for people living on the mainland

United States."[15] He wanted to set the tough and ugly story of *Thunderheart* against a spectacularly beautiful environment, to highlight the disturbing conflict between the poverty of the people and this splendid landscape.

In *Thunderheart* the FBI agent Ray Levoi played by Val Kilmer (who is part Cherokee) is chosen to investigate a murder on the reservation because he is part Indian, and in the process he discovers his ancestral roots and has a spiritual reawakening that reconnects him with the Earth and the "Old Ways." He has visions of the Indian Ghost Dance, which was performed as part of the mystical cult founded by a Paiute Indian named Wovoka, and culminated in the massacre at Wounded Knee in 1890. Graham Greene plays a tribal Sioux policeman called Crow Horse, who understands the ways of his people as Jim Chee and Dashee did in *The Dark Wind*; and Fred Ward is a corrupt tribal leader modeled after Dick Wilson, who was fighting against the American Indian Movement in the 1970's with his GOON Squad of vigilantes (Guardians of the Oglala Nation). It turns out that the militant Sioux Jimmy Looks Twice is innocent of the murder he's accused of—he's poignantly played in the film by John Trudell, the AIM spokesman whose wife and children were killed in a house fire after he delivered a speech against the FBI in 1979—and the guilty party is the FBI agent played by Sam Shepard, who's involved in a shady deal to scare property owners off uranium-rich land by poisoning the water. Similarly, in *The Dark Wind* the bad guys are the FBI narcotics agents turned drug traffickers. Apted says that during his research he discovered that the government was offering Lakota Sioux tribal leaders "half a million dollars to turn their reservation into a nuclear waste site."[16] The British director, who based his fictional story on real events that took place on the Pine Ridge Reservation between 1971 and 1978, believes it was through the covert work of the FBI that the government destroyed the American Indian Movement, which was finished by 1977, and dismantled their political voice.

Redford had become aware of the Leonard Peltier case in 1980 while talking with Peter Matthiessen, who was writing about it in his book *In The Spirit of Crazy Horse* (1983). Crazy Horse was the legendary leader of the Oglala Sioux who opposed the army order to retreat into reservations, when gold was discovered on land sacred to the Indians—the Black Hills—and formed an alliance with the Cheyenne to defeat Custer at Little Big Horn in 1876. Matthiessen told Redford that Peltier's life was in danger while he was held in the federal penitentiary in Marion, Illinois; so Redford, who had just played a prison warden committed to jail reform in *Brubaker* (1979), decided to visit Peltier in jail, "to hopefully thwart any threat against his life," and "was extremely impressed by his stature and dignity."[17]

Redford was convinced that Peltier had been unfairly sentenced to life imprisonment for having murdered two FBI agents on the Pine Ridge Reservation in 1975 and wanted to focus attention on this injustice to get him a new trial. The documentary *Incident at Oglala* does not say whether Peltier is guilty or innocent, but it presents a convincing argument that the FBI falsified evidence in order to get a jury to convict him, after two other men accused of the murders were acquitted. Redford said his interest lay in discussing "the issue hovering over the documentary: Did this man receive a fair trial in a system of justice that's gone corrupt? Do we have a double standard that slights minorities, in this case specifically Native Americans? I think yes; so that has to be looked at, because it touches on basic freedoms and rights in this country."[18] Apted says: "I personally believe that Peltier is innocent. The film doesn't make that claim. The film makes the claim that evidence was not put in front of the jury; that the government lied and tap danced around a lot of crucial evidence which they, by their own admission, withheld from the defense."[19]

There was some hope that a Redford-backed film would reopen the case, as it happened with the Errol Morris documentary *A Thin Blue Line*, which led to the exoneration of a vagabond wrongly convicted of murder; but *Incident at Oglala* did not achieve similar results. However, especially when seen in conjunction with the fictional *Thurderheart*, it sheds some light on what was going on in the Oglala Sioux Pine Ridge reservation in the 1970's, when dozens of AIM sympathizers were murdered in internecine warfare with the complicity of the FBI. Redford says of Peltier's wrongful incarceration: "The poor man was just rotting there. He may be innocent. And even if he's guilty, he probably had good cause to do what he did, considering the abuse of these people by our government. There was intimidation. It was a war zone."[20] According to Redford the reasons for the FBI's intervention had to do with supporting the greed of developers: "The abuse at Pine Ridge took place on land that the government would love to control because of the uranium and gas and oil underneath it. My position is that Hoover, in alliance with business interests, was out to protect those resources."[21] It's the same theme that he had dealt with as a director in *The Milagro Beanfield War* and as an ecologically aware developer at Sundance.

The main point is that Redford doesn't subscribe to the myth of Indians as "noble savages," but he is genuinely interested in their culture and prepared to help their cause today; by playing roles of Westerners sympathetic to the Indians, as in *Tell Them Willie Boy is Here* or *Jeremiah Johnson*, and by producing films about the injustices they suffered. He also offered concrete help by organizing meetings between tribal leaders and industries that wanted to do business on the Indian reservations, through his Institute for Resource Management founded in 1983.

11. THE HORSE WHISPERER

The Westerner as healer

In his most personal directorial effort, *The Horse Whisperer* (1998), Robert Redford also stars as a modern cowboy living on his family ranch with his brother, his brother's wife and their three boys, tending a herd of cattle and riding horses in the expansive western landscape of Montana. This film perfectly illustrates Redford's lifelong attachment to the West and the cowboy lifestyle that has been a defining element of the American character. Michael Coyne describes this phenomenon: "For the United States, the Western film and the national identity have been inextricably linked. The cowboy has been recognized world-wide as one of the most potent and enduring symbols of America."[1]

Redford had been unwilling to act in the movies he directed, preferring to cast look-alike younger protagonists, like Brad Pitt in *A River Runs Through It* and later Matt Damon in *Legend of Bagger Vance*; but he decided to play the title character in this particular case, because he felt a special kinship with material that was close to his heart. "I felt it would be comfortable to play Tom Booker because I understood a lot about him. He is appealing because of what he does, how he does it and what he stands for in his own particular life ethic. He was an absolute product of the land and the West. I felt I could bring a lot of my own experience to that character."[2]

It is significant that, when Redford decided to revisit his youthful cowboy image in his later years, he chose to portray a mature cowboy who does not engage in the juvenile sport of rodeo riding or in violent gunfights. Tom

Booker is instead a centered and thoughtful rancher who's comfortable with himself and has found his place in the world, on the saddle of a horse raising cattle in Montana country. He also has a natural gift that he was born with: he can talk to horses. When the career woman (Kristin Scott-Thomas) says, "I read this article about what you do for people with horse problems," Tom answers, "The truth is I help horses with people problems."

Disney had bought the movie rights to the first novel by British author Nicholas Evans specifically for Redford's company, Wildwood, for $3 millions, after a bidding frenzy over the still unfinished manuscript in 1994; it was Evans himself who chose Redford over other contenders. The shooting, often delayed by bad weather, started in 1996; a real working ranch was chosen for the location because of its proximity to a mountain range and the river, in an area of Montana famous not only for fly-fishing but also for horse and cattle ranching, that Redford was already familiar with having shot *A River Runs Through It* there.

The Horse Whisperer starts with a fatal accident, a scary sequence shot in jump cuts and jarring sounds. Grace (Scarlett Johansson), a privileged teenage girl, wakes up in her country home in Connecticut after dreaming of her beautiful horse, while her father Robert (Sam Neill) is still asleep, and goes for an early morning horseback ride in the snow-covered woods with her best friend Judith (Kate Bosworth). Everything is peaceful until, suddenly, Judith falls off her horse who has slipped on the icy ground, just as an out-of-control big-rig truck comes skidding down the steep mountain road; our young heroine is thrown and injured, when her horse, Pilgrim, rears up against the truck. The girl's mother, Annie MacLean (the same last name as Norman MacLean, author of the novel *A River Runs Through It* that Redford turned into a film in 1992), a busy magazine editor working in Manhattan, is summoned to the hospital, where the daughter's leg is amputated; but she refuses to let the injured horse be put down, as the veterinarian has suggested. The 13-year-old girl has trouble recovering emotionally from this trauma: she stops going to school, stays in her room watching videos of her equestrian competitions; and when she visits the horse she clearly loves and finds him spooked, she becomes even more despondent. Her laid-back father wants to give it time, but her take-charge mother decides to be more pro-active. She reads books about horses, checks the Internet, finds a magazine article about horse whisperers, calls Tom Booker on the phone; he's unwilling to help, but the determined woman is undeterred. She knows instinctually that this is the right thing to do to help her daughter recover, so, against her husband's objections, she rents a trailer and transports the intractable horse and her reluctant daughter across country from New York to Montana.

Redford the visual director utilized different color palettes for this transition from the East to the West, from dark to light, literally opening up the frame—from a 185 matte to a 235 ratio—when the two women start their trip across country, to encompass the West's open vistas. He orchestrated these visual clues with the cinematographer, Robert Richardson, who operated his own camera, and wanted them to be almost subliminal. "The overall concept of the film, photographically, for me was that I saw the East—the urban environment of New York and Connecticut in the wintertime—as dark, and that's also where the characters are most unconscious and in their dark zone. So the idea would be to begin the film with a very dark look and feeling, very compressed like the energy of the city, and as the mother and daughter move West, the film opens up. Then the light begins to change, more light comes into their lives and the healing begins; and that was easy because you moved from winter to spring to summer, where there's longer days and more light, and you're going West, where there's more space. So nature provided the landscape for us, all we had to do was be careful not to do postcard work, but to shoot the reality of the way it really looks."[3]

These visual clues are aided by the slow pace of the trip with its aerial shots of the landscape, which allows time for the viewers to calm down and open their minds to a more relaxed country lifestyle. The contrast mirrors the difference between the frenetic ways of a woman from the East Coast, who's actually an outsider from England, and the grounded man born and raised in the West, who is comfortable in his surroundings and in touch with nature. Redford, a man raised in Los Angeles California who built his own house in Utah and clearly loves the West, but also keeps an apartment in New York, is conscious of this dichotomy and careful to nuance his statement, "I didn't want to pit the West against the East. I am a Westerner in heart and nature, but there is a lot I find attractive about living in a sharp, tough urban area. It rounds out your own existence and development."[4]

Richard LaGravenese, who did a rewrite of the Eric Roth script, said he had never understood the western man, coming from an Italian background; he thought it was a myth, "this sort of unfeeling, cardboard caricature of heroism," but Redford taught him otherwise, that "the western man is a deeply feeling being, but he doesn't wear his heart on his sleeve. There's a beauty in his stoicism. The western man is so in touch with nature and the world and the earth, that he's more attuned to understanding that he is a part of the world, not in control of it; whereas an urban man suffers under the illusion, because he lives in a man-made world, that he actually can control the world, which leads to neurosis, because we can't."[5] The screenwriter says he related better to the urban woman from New York, since he was raised in Brooklyn, and Redford helped with his understanding of the western man.

This is how Redford describes the female protagonist: "Annie MacLean has an impressive and courageous energy, and I think that is a very attractive quality; yet hers is a rather blind energy because it's coming from a place she doesn't fully understand, it is sort of an unconscious and undirected energy. That's a great place to begin, with a character who is moving towards vulnerability and compassion and sensitivity. She doesn't understand herself initially, and I think in her case it was because there was no real center, there was something at the core that was missing that she needed to find."[6]

Not unlike the relationship between the cowboy and the female journalist in *Electric Horseman*, it is the man of the West who teaches the woman from the East to appreciate a lifestyle in touch with nature and to find her spirituality. Redford explains: "To me, one of the intriguing aspects about the character of Annie MacLean is the nature of her business in journalism. She is a magazine editor, which gives her the ability to bop into any place in the world, go right to the heart of a situation and presume to understand it completely. It is a kind of arrogance to take charge or try to; but the fact that she struggles and fails, that she has to relax and give up, was one of the appealing things for me."[7]

Eventually Annie, after she settles with her daughter in a guest-house on the ranch, while Tom starts his work on the horse, tries to slow down and she's no longer on the phone with her New York office at all hours; so much so that she ends up getting fired, and claims not to care anymore. She even becomes domestic, invites the Booker family over for a home-cooked meal; she nervously prepares a simple dish, spaghetti, but is fumbling in the kitchen where Tom goes to reassure her. This kind of scattered behavior is contrasted with the placid calm of the other woman in the film, Diane Booker (Dianne Wiest), the wife of Tom's younger brother Frank (Chris Cooper). She sometimes longs to get away from the drudgery of daily life on the ranch, take a trip to see some of the world—Morocco is her dream—but she knows her place as a rancher's wife and mother, this is where she belongs.

Redford recommended some books to Dianne Wiest so she could understand the mentality of a woman living on a ranch: *Riding the White Horse Home: A Western Family Album*, a 1993 memoirs by Theresa Jordan about her life on the Wyoming cattle ranch that had belonged to her family for four generations, and *The Solace of Open Spaces* by Gretel Ehrlich, a documentary filmmaker from the East Coast who became a ranch hand herding sheep and cattle in Wyoming. Jordan quotes what historian Dee Brown wrote about pioneer women, "as a mass maternal force their power was unmatched in the domestication process that transformed the wild frontiersmen into ordinary placid citizens." She also addresses the futility of Diane's longing for a trip abroad away from the ranch: "There are a few rules to ranching that mustn't be broken. One is that you rise at five-thirty each morning . . . A second rule is that ranchers don't take vacations . . . A real vacation—where we might be gone for several days or even two weeks—that was unthinkable." Ehrlich writes, "One of the myths about the West is its portrayal as a boy's world, but the women I met—descendants of outlaws, homesteaders, ranchers, and Mormon pioneers—were as tough and capable as the men were softhearted."

On the contrary, Annie, the rootless woman that lived all over the world with her diplomat father, does not know where she belongs; this is why she needs Tom, a man who is solidly rooted to the family ranch where he grew up, to calm her nervous energy and help her figure out what she really wants. In *The Horse Whisperer* there are several shots of Tom shaking his head and smiling, when he sees the woman's inappropriate white hat or her inability to keep her elegantly clad foot still; Annie even says at one point, "Why do I get the feeling that you're laughing at me?" It's the same kind of bemused comment about female frivolity that Redford had for Fonda's high-heel boots in *Electric Horseman* or Michelle Pfeiffer's clumsy behavior in *Up Close and*

Personal. While this condescending criticism of the neurotic behavior of a career woman could raise some feminist objections, Kristen Scott Thomas does not see it this way: "I don't think it's a question of being a career woman; this woman could have been doing anything and she would have been like that, it doesn't have anything to do with her job. She could be working in a bank, she could be a schoolmistress; it's not the career that's important, it's the lack of focus or the wrong focus. It's like she's racing through life to get to the end of it, and the career happens to help her go faster—she does that with her children, she does that with her husband—it's head down and get on with it. That's what the character is about, it's not the definition of a career woman; I think that the portrayal of the women in the film is very realistic and not as black-and-white and clear-cut."[8]

One morning Tom, after learning that she used to ride English-style, brings Annie a horse (and a cowboy hat) and asks her to join him for a ride; after he patiently teaches her how to get comfortable in the saddle, they spend the whole day riding in rolling meadows, reaching a bluff overlooking the valley at sunset, with the dark mountains in the background and grey storm clouds overhead. They dismount and continue an early conversation about their contrasting lifestyles; Annie had said that, not having experienced city life—with museums and restaurants, theater and music—Tom couldn't know what he was missing. Tom had revealed that he did live in Chicago where he met his wife, and now he explains that he had brought her to live in the ranch, but she had not been able to handle the open spaces and left. She was a cellist and he had fallen in love with her playing a Dvorak concerto (this is the record that we had seen him listening to in his room at night). In answer to Annie's uncertainty about having done the right thing to come here, Tom praises her courage. They get back on their horses, their dark shapes—man and woman in cowboy hats—silhouetted against the red sky. Like in *Electric Horseman* (and also in *Up Close and Personal* with Michelle Pfeiffer playing a television anchor woman), Redford plays a serious man who falls in love with a woman after learning to admire her competence in her profession and her "guts" in her personal decisions, despite his initially dismissive attitude about female frailties.

The enduring romanticism of a horseback ride in the open country is the highlight of the love story in this as in countless other films. Two other recent examples demonstrate that the fascination with western mythology persists in our culture, despite being questioned and forgotten. In *All The Pretty Horses* (2000) directed by Billy Bob Thornton from the novel by Cormac McCarthy, the American ranch-hand (Matt Damon) goes for a forbidden night-time horseback ride with the daughter (Penelope Cruz) of the Mexican landowner (Ruben Blades), confirming their love but sealing his fate. In *Down in the Valley* (2006), directed by David Jacobson, the modern cowboy (Edward Norton) "borrows" two horses to take the teenage girl (Evan Rachel Wood) for a ride in what open spaces remain in today's San Fernando Valley, as a gesture of romantic courtship. Even tough we later find out that his posturing as a cowboy is the product of a twisted mind, ultimately the beauty of his western ideals exerts a positive influence on the lives of two lost teenagers, the girl and his younger brother (Rory Culkin).

In *Horse Whisperer*, the cowboy develops a fatherly relationship with the teenage girl, involving her in the work he's doing with the horse, encouraging her to find the self-confidence to ride Pilgrim again, her disability no longer blocking her; he also teaches her to drive his truck, to prove that she can do things she's afraid to try. Tom wants to find out what exactly happened during the accident that injured her, and eventually Grace tearfully tells him; he explains that, by rearing up against the big truck, Pilgrim was trying to protect her, because he loved her "so damn much." While the horse slowly learns to trust his leader, who is showing infinite patience and understanding, the girl heals as well, helping with the cattle branding and cleaning up after the horses. In a dramatic scene, the horse whisperer decides to tie up the horse's leg, forcing him to lie down, then he sits on top of him asking a frightened Grace to sit next to him; it is this proof that they don't intend to harm him that convinces the horse to let the girl ride him again. Under the eyes of her proud father who has comes to visit, Grace triumphantly raises her arms as she rides Pilgrim inside the round corral in slow motion.

Redford says that the mother-daughter relationship was especially interesting to him, and he creates several insightful arguments between the two women who are able to reconcile in the end by recognizing their similarities. Annie says she also felt all alone after her father died when she was twelve, reassuring Grace that one day somebody will love her. Scarlett Johansson says that, in her depression and anguish, Grace is worried, "being so young and having a whole future ahead of her," that nobody is going to love her because of her disability; "she feels like a total failure, and that she will never live up to her mother's expectations of a perfect child."[9] Redford says about Johansson playing Grace, "I knew she should be feisty, because I wanted to be able to have her be some sort of duplication of the mother, with neither one of them really knowing it or wanting it, but they're a bit cut from the same cloth. The fact that Johansson is an urban child brought a lot to it, because she's a 13-year-old going on 40; so I thought that would give her real combative strength toward the mother, she'd go after the mother and she'd be real tough."[10]

As Redford probably witnessed in his own family—in the relationship between his wife and two daughters—this is a typical phase that most families go through, when the daughter, moving from childhood into adolescence, needs to differentiate herself from the other woman in the family that she had modeled herself after, and becomes closer to her father, eventually overcoming this angst and making peace with the mother. In the end Grace realizes that it was her mother who made her recovery possible in the first place, by leaving her high-powered job as a magazine editor in Manhattan, taking her to Montana and staying there for months until she and her horse were both healed.

On a parallel line, Tom and Annie had gotten closer, they had kissed and embraced in a moonlit encounter by the river during a cattle drive; but now that Tom has met her husband, he's reluctant to go further, questions whether she really knows what she wants, reiterates that the ranch is where he belongs. In the book their love affair is consummated and Annie finds out later, after returning home to her husband, that she's going to have a baby. But Redford decided not to go in that direction, he shows Tom behaving as a mature man, encouraging the confused woman to think about the pain she might inflict on her family. He explains: "I was planning to carry forward the idea that they had an affair, but as we started to film it, there was this voice that kept haunting me, that a truer and tougher road, a more bittersweet but more honest approach to that ending would be if they made this choice of knowing that it could not work. So why go down a road where a lot of people would be affected and hurt, especially the girl?"[11] A family man with a son and two daughters, Redford probably knew all too well the emotional toll that a divorce can exert on teenagers; his youngest,

Amy, was 15 when he separated from his wife Lola in 1985, shortly before his love affair with Sonia Braga on the set of *The Milagro Beanfield War*. So the director created a scene of intense but repressed love, when Tom and Annie have a heart-breaking slow dance at a country fair, looking into each other's eyes, his hand hugging her lower back, her hand squeezing his shoulder; but they cannot go further because her husband is sitting in the room. In the end, having understood the rightfulness of his wisdom, it is the woman who leaves the man, riding home in her Range Rover pulling the horse trailer, while the cowboy on horseback watches her from a bluff.

This is in contrast to the ending of Redford's first Western *Tell Them Willie Boy Is Here*, where the cowboy walks away into the sunset, but it's similar to ending of *Electric Horseman*, where the mismatched couple have one last night of lovemaking, but know that they have to separate; the woman returns to her work as a journalist and the man manages to escape the media glare and release the horse free in the wild.

A recent Western, *Open Range* (2003) written and directed by Kevin Costner, shows the opposite kind of male-female relationship; it's the woman from the East (Annette Bening) who convinces the once-violent cowboy (Kevin Costner) to leave his meandering lifestyle of cattle drives to settle in the town and get married. His older boss and mentor (Robert Duvall) reveals that he once had a wife who was killed, and that is why he chose the life on the open range; but he encourages his protégé to give settled family life a chance.

To better understand Redford's reluctance to condone adultery on the part of a married woman, we can refer to his feelings about a man cheating on his wife, a role he played in *The Clearing* (2004). In this thriller, when a businessman is kidnapped by a disgruntled former employee (Willem Dafoe), his wife (Helen Mirren) discovers that he was having an affair; but Redford says that "somebody having another relationship does not necessarily mean they don't love the person," and that the film was not about this man's betrayal, but about somebody who had lost their perspective because of the greed typical of American society. "This man was drifting apart from his wife because he was obsessed with following the American dream of money and success, to the point where you're constantly driving yourself to that extra dollar, and you start to lose connections with other parts of yourself, like your family and your wife . . . And the extramarital affair happened because he was in an unconscious lost place where he didn't feel like he could really communicate to his wife anymore."[12] Through long hours of fear and emotional anguish, finally he understands what he has lost and writes a love letter to his wife, even though he will never see her again. "When the crisis comes, and he's in a life-and-death situation, he's forced to really look hard at his life and what it means; and he discovers a lot of things that he had missed, including how much he really loved her and how much her drift was caused by him."[13] While the regret about being unfaithful is punished by death in this instance, Redford had not found it necessary to go to that extreme in *The Horse Whisperer*.

Another difference between the film and the novel is that Tom Booker doesn't die, and Redford explains why: "I felt it was a tougher film if the characters had to live with their sacrifices rather than being let off the hook by death."[14] In the novel Evans describes in gruesome detail how the man who talked to horses was killed by them, after getting between two fighting stallions to protect Grace from being hurt. The writer feels that Redford's ending "completely missed the point of the book. Although Tom Booker is a real character, there is an important mythological aspect to him. He is an immortal, the redemptive angel, the man in the white hat. There is a rule about such characters: when their work is done, they have to move on. Of course, he will live on forever in their hearts—and in the new child that is born at the end of the story."[15]

Despite these different sensibilities, there were many elements that were interesting to Redford in Evans' novel, even though he didn't ultimately like the way it developed, after having read a manuscript still without an ending. "I choose to do it because as an actor there was a good role that I could play and bring some credibility to, and then the whole piece had all the elements that I would be attracted to as a director. I mean, the journey to discovery, the mythological proportion of the piece, having to do with primal things like mother-daughter relationships, the journey from darkness to light, from unconsciousness to consciousness, from East to West; all that was very attractive to me. The complexity of human relationships and family dynamics, particularly when people are dealing with conscious and unconscious situations, are an endlessly interesting terrain for me to mine from; it also had the physicality of a part of the country I love and know pretty well, as well as I know New York."[16]

Redford was so intrigued by the protagonist because he saw him as a hero, a spiritual healer: "I think that people want to believe that a man like Tom Booker exists in the world; in our culture we've lost most of our heroes, our mythology is getting away from us. I think heroes touch something higher and they bring it back as a gift to the people, then they're usually destroyed for it. Tom Booker is a hero because he heals and he saves the soul . . . , but it doesn't mean that heroes are perfect or that they themselves are not in need of some kind of healing. In my interpretation of heroism, is that it always comes with some sacrifice. I find that more interesting than the cowboy in the white hat who shoots ten people, blows on his barrel, moves on and plays cards."[17]

The god-given gift of healing makes the Horse Whisperer resemble an Indian Shaman. The film title refers to a technique of healing and training horses—although the real-life practitioners of this art reject the term "horse-whisperer"—that originated in ancient Scotland to describe people who seemed to have an almost spiritual rapport with horses.

The "Horse Whisperers" movement, which is more appropriately called "Natural Horsemanship," was pioneered by two brothers from Oregon who settled in California's Carmel Valley in the 1930s: Bill (1906-1999) and Tom Dorrance (1910-2003). There they embraced the Mexican vaquero tradition of non-violent horse training, also favored by American Indians. As Tom said in his 1987 book *True Unity: Willing Communication Between Horse and Human*, "Listen to the horse. Try to find out what the horse is trying to tell you."

The traditional western technique of "breaking" horses relies on forcing the animal into submission through fear, implying a violent domination of man over beast. In contrast, the natural method of "gentling" horses is based on earning the trust of the animal in non-violent ways, creating a friendly empathy, but still establishing the human as the leader that the horse naturally seeks in a herd. Jane Smiley, author of the novel *Horse Heaven* (2000), says: "The method originated in Tom's detailed observations of how horses in herds interact . . . to communicate to one another . . . The Dorrance method is never based on force or fear . . . Such a process transforms the human-equine relationship from . . . fearful and conflict-driven . . . into something more like a partnership."[18]

This method, sometimes called "resistance-free" or "gentle" training, was also employed by Idaho cowboy Ray Hunt (born in 1929) who wrote a book called *Think Harmony With Horses* (1991). He insisted on training a horse without humiliating it, but rather by trying to become friends with him: "Always offer him the best deal possible. Never make a horse do something he doesn't want to do . . . The horse is entitled to his opinion, I'm the one who came into his world, uninvited. And if I was asking a lady to dance with me, I would sure get her permission first. If I get kicked, it isn't his fault, it's my fault; we're supposed to be the ones with brains."[19] The key to getting along with a horse, Ray believes, is patience, respect and understanding.

The "Horse Whisperer" tradition was continued by Ray disciple Buck Brannaman, the Wyoming trainer who inspired Evans' novel and served as technical advisor on Redford's film. Another horse whisperer, Monty Roberts (born in 1935)—author of *The Man Who Listens to Horses* (1997) and subject of the BBC documentary *Monty Roberts: Real Horse Whisperer*—claims that Nicholas Evans visited his Flag Is Up Farm in Solvang California to discuss his "Join Up" method of "starting" not "breaking" horses and based 70 percent of the novel on his life, but that he refused to cooperate with the film production because he objected to a scene where Redford tied up one of the horse's leg and forced him to lie down. Both Redford and Evans deny his claim.

Brannaman (born in Wisconsin in 1963 and raised in Montana, he now lives in Sherydan, Wyoming), author of *The Faraway Horses* (2002), says it's not natural for a horse to accept that a human will throw a saddle over him and jump on his back, in fact this puts him on the defensive. As somebody who was abused as a child by his drunken dad, then raised by a kinder family of ranchers, Brannaman wrote: "Showing your horse who's boss by sticking a spur in him or whipping him won't work. Force and violence never do. If horses are going to survive in our world, someone must lay down rules and then be persevering and disciplined enough to follow through. The same is true for kids."[20] He doesn't even use the word "break" in his work, he calls it "colt starting," and it begins with developing a "kinship" so that horse and rider come to trust each other. This is how Brannaman describes the purpose of the clinics that he has been teaching for horse owners since 1980: "I'm really just trying to get them to understand where the horse is coming from, how the horse perceives things, what it takes for him to learn. I want them to go away with some empathy for the horse."[21]

This enlightened way of treating horses rooted in the West has now become a standard around the world, where it has influenced every discipline of horse training, including the much older tradition of English-style dressage. Queen Elizabeth II invited Monty Roberts to demonstrate his method in 1989 and later hired him to train the horses of the Royal family.

In the film *Horse Whisperer* Annie Maclean reads in voice-over from a book about the history of horses' relations with men. Redford explains how this ancient understanding between the two species is reflected in the beliefs of American Indians: "There's an effort in the film to show this anthropological history of horses for the audience's benefit, to remind them of how it started; it wasn't this way until human beings came in and decided to try to convert the animal into submission for their own use, either for meat or for slavery; that's when the trouble started; but up to that point there was a different relationship. The Native Americans lived with animals in a different way, because of their relationship with animals and what they believed about the animals' place on earth, that is the same as their own pretty much; then things were okay. So this language that's spoken by the whisperer is a language that understands that original connection of beast to human, rather than beating the animal, kicking it and intimidating it, it acknowledges a relationship through trust; and there's a language for that and there's a way with that, and it takes patience. We tried to illustrate that by a scene where I go out and I wait for the horse to come to me, I wait for hours and hours and just stay still, so that we slowly make this connection. That can't be done by that many people, you have to have a very strong energy inside you, almost a spiritual kind of energy, that sends a strong signal to a horse, that the horse will pick up; and not everyone has that."[22]

As in *Electric Horseman*, where the horse symbolized the better self of the protagonist as played by Redford, in *Horse Whisperer* as well the special relationship between the horse and the cowboy signifies that this is a man who lives in harmony with nature. Redford explains: "My character is at one with himself and the land, and animals being a part of that environment, he developed an ability to take that oneness into an art, into a skill, into a job for himself; he's working with animals. That came out of a gift that he was born with, but also the environment he grew up in, where people who work very close to nature are going to be very close to animals; one way or another you have to develop a way to be with animals. The old way to deal with a horse was to beat him into submission, but Tom Booker had developed a new technique based on an understanding and a compassion, and, of course, that could be translated to human beings as well. It all came from the combination of him having a special gift of sensitivity and understanding—while still being a pretty tough guy, because you have to be tough to live and work in the West—and what he learned as he developed his skill. As he went on, he learned more about how to communicate with animals and, when you do that, you send to the animal a message of trust, and once the animal receives that message that you're not going to hurt him, then in turn he returns that gesture by faith and then a relationship develops that leads to a certain kind of harmony."[23] He adds, "The term 'horse whispering' is a kind of euphemism for a state of being, a relationship between a human and a horse. It's about understanding who you are and respecting your place with one another. To have that kind of acceptance requires a certain degree of spirituality."[24]

As an amusing aside we notice that years later Redford, who is the grandfather of four children, would agree to lend his voice to Ike the grumpy horse in the animated version of *Charlotte's Web* (2006) starring Dakota Fanning, based on the 1952 children's classic by E. B. White.

When it comes to a more enlightened relationships between man and horses, an appropriate example of the changed *Zeitgeist* in popular culture is the animated film *Spirit: Stallion of the Cimarron* (2002), written not coincidentally by John Fusco who had penned *Young Guns* (1988) and *Thunderheart* (1992) and will later write *Hidalgo* (2004). Produced by Jeffrey Katzenberg at DreamWorks, *Spirit* is the story of a wild mustang (voiced by Matt Damon with songs by Bryan Adams) raised in the Old West who roams as free as an eagle—the animation showing a bird's eye view of mythical western landmarks from Monument Valley to the Grand Canyon, from Yosemite to Yellowstone. His happy life as leader of the herd comes to an end when he's captured by the U.S. Cavalry and taken to the fort, where the soldiers attempt to "break" him but are all throw off by an increasingly defiant animal. The angry Colonel punishes the unruly horse by ordering him tied to a post for three days without food and water. A young Lakota brave, who had himself been captured, helps Spirit escape, freeing all the other horses from the fort in the process, and shows him affection, teaching him, with his playful way of treating his own horse, a fetching mare, that genuine friendship can exist between humans and animals. In the end the horse, by disrupting the railroad that is pointed toward his beloved West, becomes a symbol of the untamed spirit of the West resisting the advance of "civilization."

John Fusco, who lives with his family on a horse farm in Vermont, became passionate about preserving the Spanish mustangs while researching *Thunderheart* on the Pine Ridge Reservation of South Dakota. These descendents of Hiberic horses—that were brought to America by Cortéz in the early 1500s—are a small but hardy breed; they were eventually adopted by the Indian tribes and are sometime called "Indian ponies," but they have now become virtually extinct. Fusco says that there was a government campaign to exterminate Indian horses, that General Custer shot 800 Indian ponies; he has Chief Eagle Horne make this point in *Hidalgo*, "The buffalo herds have been destroyed, the elk and deer are gone, now the government is rounding up our wild horses and planning to shoot them too."

Fusco also heard from the Lakotas stories about Frank T. Hopkins, the legendary western rider who in 1890 competed with his mustang in the Ocean of Fire race covering 3000 miles of Arabian desert. Even though the historic accuracy of this race has been questioned, Viggo Mortensen who plays Hopkins in the film says that he believes Fusco's research, because unconnected Indian tribes in different reservations—the Lakotas in South Dakota and the Blackfeet in Montana—are told the same oral legends by their grandparents. Fusco says that Hopkins was "a knowledgeable horseman and an acknowledged distance rider, an early proponent of mustang preservation," and that "his legend lives as folklore in that world, and still inspires, no matter what the truth is."[25]

Hopkins, at least in the legendary retelling of his adventures in *Hidalgo*, was part Indian—his father being an Army Corporal and his mother a Lakota chief's daughter—and his Indian name was Blue Child; that is one reason why he has such a friendly rapport with his horse, treats him like a partner, calls him "brother." As a dispatch rider for the U.S. Cavalry he delivers the order to disarm a Lakota encampment, and he explains to the worried soldiers that it's not an uprising, but a Ghost Dance, the Indians are praying to their ancestors; but they are massacred anyway, at Wounded Knee in 1890. This tragic event, for which he feels partly responsible, is what drives Hopkins to turn into a drunken cowboy, while performing with his horse in *Buffalo Bill's Wild West Show*, before his pride is restored when he's invited as a dare to compete in the Arabian race and performs heroic deeds, not only winning over fierce competition but rescuing the Sheikh's daughter.

Fusco says that we have lost our connection with horses, we forgot how important they were for our cultural development, as part of our heritage; he particularly would like to see young Native Americans reconnect to the descendants of their grandfathers' horses, reeducate children and teenagers who don't know about their history with this animal to care for the horses.

In Indian mythology the horse is considered a sacred animal, every tribe has a legend as to how they acquired the horse from their holy beings. In his book, *When Indians Became Cowboys*, Peter Iverson says that it was the Spaniards who brought the horse to the new world—the Spanish vaqueros that entered Arizona and New Mexico with Francisco Vásquez de Coronado in 1540 depended on the horse to round up cattle; but in the 1600s Indian tribes like the Apache and the Comanche and other tribes in the Southwest began to covet and acquire horses. The Navajo (Diné) have a legend about the White Bead Woman chanting of different color mares coming from the East and West, the North and the South, and transforming four stone fetishes into living horses. The deity also explained that the parts of the animal related to the elements, the hair of the mane and tail to the streaks of rain, the ears to heat lightening, the eyes to the big stars.

With *The Horse Whisperer* Redford clearly illustrates the full range of his feelings about the enduring values of the American West, the fast-disappearing lifestyle of a real present-day cowboy, not a mythological movie icon; and that was his conscious intention. "The film provided me with the opportunity to show the West not only as it used to be as a way of life, but as it still is in very small pockets. The times we live in are changing so quickly and we mostly have a very synthetic existence. It's almost an anomaly to find real ranch life anymore, or to see it as a way of life where ranchers live in accordance with nature, reaping what they live on, crop by crop and season by season. It was interesting for me to focus on a family that still lives the way they lived 100 years ago, where they farm or ranch the land and yield a crop that sustains them. It was appealing to capture that realistically, not just in seeing technically how they do it, but as much about their behavior, their lifestyle and the ethic and philosophy of that way of life."[26] Redford also touches on another theme close to his heart: his ecological concerns for the preservation of a natural way of life threatened by machines and greedy oil companies or real-estate developers. "Most of the origins of the American cowboy came out of two places, outlaws and homesteaders . . . the real cowboy was tied to a real situation, someone who had to work the land in order to make a living. And that's less and less possible because of the economic situation in the United States. It used to be mining and timber-cutting that pushed that person out, now real estate developers are pretty well pushing the cowboy out of existence."[27] He had explored the theme of farmers' livelihood threatened by resort developers in The Milagro Beanfield War and had fought against the building of roads and power plants in the Utah wilderness close to his home.

Other recent Westerns eulogize the cowboy way of life of raising cattle on horseback, but they are set in the past, in the years after World War II, when this traditional lifestyle became threatened by changing economic realities and stopped being financially viable.

In Hi-Lo Country (1999), directed by Stephen Frears from the 1961 novella by Max Evans, screenplay by Walon Green, two friends from New Mexico return from World War II to their old way of life; they call their trade "cowboying." Resisting the buy-out offers of a big rancher (Sam Elliott) who tells them that "only in the movies" people still drive cattle to the railheads rather than transporting it by truck, and encouraged by the high price of beef, they decide to buy and raise their own cattle. As Pete (Billy Crudup) the introspective narrator says, "The pure simple joy of a cattle drive, all that sky, all that land stretching out toward the horizon. There's no sense of freedom that ever sets a man so high, makes him feel, yes, this is what I was born to do." Understanding the inextricable connection between herding cows and riding on horseback, the cowboys are also full of praise for their horses, and they love them as much as their women. Pete admires Big Boy (Woody Harrelson), the extroverted boisterous cowboy, for his casual way with horses; Big Boy compares a good woman to a good horse, "they will not let you down when you get into that old bind," and they will work their heart out for you on a cattle drive. Max Evans, who served in Europe during World War II and described his own ranching experiences through Pete's character, says that Frears captured the modern-era West, when the advent of television, radio and the pickup truck changed the cowboy's life forever; but that cowboys are not gone, "they're still out there busting their butts, riding through the brush and breaking those horses."[28] *Hi-Lo Country* is a tribute to the classic Westerns by John Ford and Howard Hawks from an Englishman, who, like many Europeans that came of age in the 1950s, loves the genre but has an outsider's perspective. The historical time-frame resembles *Comes a Horseman* (1979) by Alan Pakula, which was also about a World War II veteran (James Caan) returning home to Montana to a changed West, joining forces with another small ranch-owner (Jane Fonda) to fight a take-over by a villainous big rancher (Jason Robards); all three ranches, however, are threatened by a voracious oilman.

In *All The Pretty Horses* (2000) directed by Billy Bob Thornton from the novel by Cormac McCarthy—which is part of his *Border Trilogy* covering the same period of transition, the late 1940s—a young man (Matt Damon) from Texas loses his right to the family farm in 1949, when his grandfather dies and his divorced mother sells it to the oil company. He decides to leave for Mexico with his best friend (Henry Thomas), because they still have big ranches down there; so they get on their horses and ride out into the expanse of the western landscape. When they meet some vaqueros herding cows, while crossing the Rio Grande, they ask for a job and distinguish themselves with their skill at breaking wild horses. After many tragic adventures, the cowboy returns home, but not before rescuing his friend's horse and bringing it back to him. Thornton says: "This movie is really about the end of the West, the end of a time in America. It's 1949 and everything was coming in, television, and the ranches were going away; and this kid represents the dying West."[29] This is how Matt Damon explains it: "The movie takes place in 1949 and it's about a time that's changing, an era that's ending. My character is trying to hang on to this way of life that he believes in and that he loves, that his grandfather and his grandfather's grandfather lived, in a society that is moving past that and advancing. He decides to go down to Mexico because the land is not all fenced in and sold off and played out down there, the cowboy way of life is still alive, it's not like it is up here in the United States."[30]

To conclude, with *The Horse Whisperer* Redford has given us a thoughtful meditation on the enduring values of the cowboy lifestyle: his connection with nature, his love for horses, and his spiritual centeredness. He has taken the mythology of the West in a different direction from the classic western themes—the six-gun fights, the barroom brawls, the prostitutes with a heat of gold, the villainous ranchers—to present a portrait of the modern cowboy hero as a healer of animals and people.

12. AN UNFINISHED LIFE

An old rancher finds forgiveness

In his mid-sixties (he was 65 when the film was made in 2003) Redford gave what many critics have called the best performance of his career in a role that seemed tailor made for him; he played an aging cowboy in *An Unfinished Life* (2005) directed by Lasse Hallström from a novel by Mark Spraggs.

Einar Gylkison lives on his ranch in Wyoming with his old army buddy and farmhand Mitch (Morgan Freeman)—in the book it's explained how they had met during the Korean War—but now Mitch needs daily care because a year previous he had been mauled by a bear. So we see the scruffy old cowboy behave like an affectionate nurse, giving his friend a daily shot of morphine on his butt, massaging his scarred back, bringing him lunch and playing cards (cribbage) with him at night. He's also tending house, getting up early in the morning to milk the lone cow, feeding stray cats, fixing sandwiches. Einar will later explain the empty corrals: he had to sell the cattle in order to keep the place, when Mitch was injured and could no longer help him with the chores; but his bitterness comes from a darker tragedy. After his daughter-in-law Jean (Jennifer Lopez), running away from an abusive relationship, shows up at his door with her 11-year-old daughter Griff (Becca Garner) and reveals that he has a grandchild he didn't know about, we find out why Einar is so angry: he blames her for his son's death in a car accident 12 years prior. He has never gotten over it and every day visits his grave on a hilltop to talk to "his boy;" the tombstone reads "Griffin Gylkison, an unfinished life, 1971-1993."

Mark Spraggs, who co-wrote the screenplay with his wife Virginia, calls the film "a strong family drama about forgiveness, how a family can be so torn apart by a tragedy and then brought back together again."[1] This journey to forgiveness is precisely what attracted Redford to the project; he could identify with a man of the West devastated by the death of his son (Redford's first child, a boy named Scott, died of sudden infant death syndrome in 1959). "I'm very attached to the character I played. Not that he's me, but I know that person by association, especially if you've spent any time in the Western states. He's so riven with bitterness and anger. Being able to take that character from being blocked emotionally to forgiveness was wonderful."[2]

Redford was also looking forward to working with a European director who had an outsider's perspective on the American West. Lasse Hallström says: "Even if this is the Wild West, I know these people, I've met them, despite the fact that the culture is so far off from where I came from. I think I know their emotions and their shortcomings, so it's a universal story on an emotional level; even a Swede can understand it." Redford says the director allowed him to collaborate on the tone of the film, so it wouldn't get too sentimental, and observes that, being a Swede, he liked things more stoic, more expressed than talked about. "I liked his sensitivity and sensibility as a filmmaker. I had faith that Lasse would leave a lot to be played between the lines, which is really customary in western life. It's a life with not a lot of words about families because the work is so hard; you live by your word and a code of honor."[3]

Clearly it was the opportunity to deal with the theme of the modern West that most interested Redford, a way to further the development of his western characters from Jeremiah Johnson to the Horse Whisperer, present a portrait of the kind of man he idealizes and understands: the strong, unsentimental, taciturn loner who eventually warms up to family connections.

It takes a young girl—still a tomboy at age 11—to open Einar's heart and find a way out of his stubborn refusal to live in the present, not clinging to the memories of his dead boy. Redford as Einar slowly develops a relationship with Griff similar to the one Tom Booker had with Grace in *The Horse Whisperer*; this time he's the grandfather not the father figure, but he's still a teacher. He shows her some of the skills needed on a ranch, how to milk a cow, how to rope a steed (it's actually Mitch's foot); and he takes her riding on his horse, when she expresses the desire to be a cowgirl. By teaching the girl about the western lifestyle, the old man remembers what he had once enjoyed about it himself. The final test of this broken cowboy's regained manhood is when he attacks the abusive boyfriend who had followed her mother and grabbed the girl; dismounting from his horse, Einar blows up the tires of the man's car with his rifle, smashes the window, grabs him by the hair and punches him in the face. He's after all a man with a violent past, like many cowboy heroes in western films. In the novel it's explained how Einar had nearly killed a man in a barroom fight for calling Mitch a nigger, in the film he comes to the aid of a waitress friend when two drunken guys mistreat her and hits them in the face with a coffee pot. It is not gratuitous violence, of course, but justified behavior when protecting your own friends and family.

Redford relished showing his age in *An Unfinished Life*, an older version of his character in *The Horse Whisperer.* "The idea of playing a crusty guy who'd gone to seed, after having played a rancher who was healthy and took care of horses, a good and solid guy, was very appealing."[4] Einar has a scraggly growth of beard, unkept hair under a shapeless brown hat, worn jeans and boots, rumpled checkered shirts; Redford says he even gained weight for the role to acquire a round belly. He's no longer the elegantly dressed cowboy of *The Horse Whisperer*, with his tight jeans covered by shiny brown leather chaps, his impeccably ironed shirt and a shining white Stetson.

Redford had always railed against critics that called him a pretty boy or a movie star thereby dismissing his acting abilities, and now he gets his revenge. No longer young in real life, he is not worried about growing old, only "of not being much use," as Tom had said to Grace in *The Horse Whisperer.* "I'm not afraid of aging because that's just a fact of life that you're going to be living with, unless you go to some drastic length to try to arrest it, as some people do; and that's not for me. But it's really what comes with aging that you look at, such as of not being of some use. I like being of use and I also like being physical; it's just the way it always was with me. I could have been somebody that was purely mental, but I like sports; I was athletic as a kid and I like being able to command my body to do what I want it to do, so I like to ski and ride horses and swim, all that.

When the time comes where growing old takes you to that place where you can't either be of use and contribute something to the world around you, through your work, or command your body to do what it loves to do, then it can get a little tricky."[5] Obviously he's not at that point yet, he's only pretending to be old in *An Unfinished Life* and it's called acting.

Actually Redford had been practicing playing disappointed older men facing retirement for some time. In *Spy Game* (2001) directed by Tony Scott he's a CIA agent at the end of his career who decides to break the rules of his organization to rescue his former protégé (Brad Pitt) from a Chinese jail; in *The Last Castle* (2001) directed by Rod Lurie he's a general who's been stripped of his command and sent to a military jail, where he leads a prisoners' revolt against an cruel warden. In both cases Redford portrays people who had played by the rules their whole lives, but in the end they respond to a higher moral imperative at a heavy personal cost. He explains the ending of *Spy Games*: "The fact that a character breaks his own rules to save the life of another is a human gesture, and I think anyone feels good when they see that, but he gives up everything that he's saved for to do it: his money, his retirement."[6] He comments on both characters: "These men are not retired, they're in the process of coming to the end of a certain career, which would be more appropriate for my age; but I'm not retiring, you know, these films are not autobiographical."[7] However, he identifies with the rebellious spirit of men who go up against an unjust and controlling system: "I've always been interested in characters that begin to go against the system that controls our lives, because it's turned corrupt or deceitful or becomes about something else, that no longer represents what it's supposed to represent in terms of the peoples' interest: the CIA and the military in this case."[8] Redford obviously still loves being an outlaw, an outsider, an original thinker; and he's not ready to retire. When he was presented with the Kennedy Center Honor (in December 2005, for his "extraordinary support of independent film, that has had an immeasurable impact on filmmakers and audiences"), he commented: "You suddenly feel like you're being bronzed. I don't feel ready for that yet, myself. I've got some nice projects ahead. In no way do I feel in the mood to retire."[9]

A central metaphor in *An Unfinished Life* is the bear, an animal that symbolizes the freedom of a natural life lived in the wild not in the cages of civilization; it's not the old horse or the lone cow that represent this concept in the film, but a young grizzly bear that wanders off the mountain in search of food raiding the small town's trash cans. Einar gets on his horse and is ready to shoot him with his rifle, when the sheriff (Josh Lucas) stops him; the bear ends up caged in a small zoo. It is the same bear—"my bear" Mitch calls him—that wounded his friend. This episode is the cause of Einar's guilt, because he was too drunk to come to his aid in time, when they stumbled upon the bear feeding on a calf one night. Mitch explains later that he holds no grudges, because the bear "was just doing what bears do, we can't punish him for that," it was they who interrupted his dinner; and he now asks Einar to set him free, get him out of that cage. A reluctant Einar cannot refuse his friend's request, so he starts teaching the girl how to drive his pick-up truck to accomplish their escape plan. This had already been a part of his purpose of showing Griff how to gain confidence in herself, and he had probably done it with his son as well when he was young; it's the same thing Tom does with Grace in *Horse Whisperer* when he teaches her to drive his truck, something that his brother's boys had been doing from a young age. When Jean observes that her daughter is 11, Einar says, "It's a ranch." Driving and fixing a truck are part of the skills needed when living on a ranch raising cows on horseback; and Redford is happy to display the reality of that lifestyle on film once more, defending its right to exist against the encroaching of business interests. "The life of ranchers has now become almost obsolete, and agriculture, a foundation of our culture, is being pushed aside by things like technology and real estate."[10]

The bear also represents the idea that each character has to face and overcome their own demons, as Jennifer Lopez says, "The bear is what we all wrestle with. Everybody has their bear in life. It's about conquering that bear and letting him go."[11] Redford had been chased by an overexcited bear up a tree while filming *Jeremiah Johnson* in 1972 and wasn't looking forward to doing this again—he doesn't believe wild animals can ever be tamed—but he trusted the trainer and decided to "throw caution to the wind" and confront the 9-feet tall grizzly, "not the most comfortable place to be."[12] Mitch also meets the bear after he has been freed—he comes growling at him—but he stands his ground, looks him the eye and the bear moves on toward his mountain retreat. The morality of liberating an imprisoned animal to allow him to roam free in the wild, which is his natural habitat, was also the theme of *Electric Horseman,* and it has a similar symbolic meaning here. The idea of the bear as a beast inhabiting someone's soul, as in ancient Indian beliefs, was also explored in Edward Zwick's *Legends of the Fall* (1994). The Ute Indians living in parts of Utah, Colorado, New Mexico and Wyoming venerated a bear spirit, who occasionally went on killing sprees; to this day each spring the Utes hold their traditional Bear Dances.

An intriguing theme of *An Unfinished Life* is that, like in *Horse Whisperer,* Redford plays a man dealing with issues between mother and daughter, a subject he knows something about, having two daughters himself, and that he has been interested in exploring. At first Einar is angry at Jean; he chastises her for her promiscuity, like a puritanical father, "Are you screwing Crane Curtis for protection or sport? Do you want to ask your daughter how she feels about it?" But eventually, as he begins to love Griff, the granddaughter named after his dead son Griffin, he pays a compliment to the way her mother has raised her, "She's a good girl. Good kids don't get that way by accident." Einar had also blamed Jean for his wife leaving him for another man, a year after his son's death, because in his grief he had stopped paying attention to her; in the book the wife is also dead, her tomb next to the son's, but here the filmmakers wanted to underline Einar's responsibility in his own demise. He finally comes to the point of forgiving Jean for being drunk, that night when she fell asleep at the wheel and his son was killed, just like he forgives Griff for hitting the gear shift while freeing the bear and putting him in danger; this is how he learns to forgive himself for being "falling down" drunk when Mitch was attacked by the bear. Redford understands the predicament of this stubborn man: "Einar goes into a retreat where he can't grow or forgive, which creates a wall around him. Forgiving in this case means admitting that you might be wrong, and that's tough for certain people."[13]

It is Mitch who voices the conscience of the piece, the wisdom he has acquired now that he's close to death, when he says in the ending, as the camera soars to show the green valley dotted with pine trees against the mountains, "I got so high I could see where the blue turns to black. From up there you can see all there is, and it looked like there was a reason for everything." Earlier he had explained to Einar why he shouldn't accuse his daughter-in-law of killing his son, "It was an accident, they call them accidents because it's nobody's fault," to which a bitter Einar had retorted, "No, they call them accidents to make the guilty feel better." Morgan Freeman, who would play a similar character, an injured old boxer giving wise advice to his old friend, in Clint Eastwood's *Million Dollar Baby* (2004)—shot later but released earlier—says about the mauling by the bear: "A physical trauma like that creates a change in you, a very vigorous hard-working man all of a sudden is very close to useless. After a year of reflection, he's probably not the same guy he used to be, he's had a lot of time to think and put things into perspective. My feelings were that he had sort of mellowed way down and watched his friend sort of deteriorate along with him."[14] Spragg explains: "We're exceedingly captivated by older men, their essential wisdom and their having carried the burden of a very long life."[15] The moral of the film is in that last phrase, that from a place of wisdom acquired by the end of your life, you can see the harmony of all things in this world. It's not unlike the ending of *A River Runs Through It*, "Eventually all things merge into one, and the river runs through it." Redford acknowledges this similarity between *An Unfinished Life* and the slow pace of his own films: "The film is very different from the normal kind of films that are coming out right now, so full of high-tech and slam-bam technical stuff, in the sense that it allows an audience to reflect as it moves. It does have the kind of flow of a river flowing."[16]

Another interesting element of *An Unfinished Life* is the relationship between the two aging cowboys who had almost become like an old married couple. It's a humorous moment when Griff observes, "I had a music teacher who was a lesbian. You guys are gay, right?" The men burst out laughing and make jokes about it; when Griff adds, "It's cool, everybody needs love," Mitch agrees, "You got that part right, little girl." This is a wink at the underlying homoeroticism of buddy Westerns, and an acknowledgment that homosexual love has become acceptable in contemporary society.

A recent example where this subject is addressed in a bawdy and light-hearted manner is *Hi-Lo Country* (1999), the Western directed by Stephen Frears. The macho man of the couple, Big Boy, says to the more effeminate Pete, when they're about to enlist during World War II, "You don't need a wife, hell you need a husband. You could send him to war and stay home to do the dishes and crochet." After their return, he reiterates his best friend's need for his male influence, "What did they do to you in the army, take the cowboy out of you? Lucky I'm back, leave you too much longer to yourself you'll be squatting to take a piss." Both men are also lusting after the same married woman; Big Boy actually sleeps with her, while Pete has to hide his repressed desire.

We had already discussed the mirroring of two men's desire for each other in the figure of a woman they both love, in reference to *Butch Cassidy and the Sundance Kid*. Feminist and Queer film theorists had explained that dynamic in the 1970s, but not until *Brokeback Mountain* (2005) by Ang Lee would real physical love between two male cowboys enjoying each other's company and relieving their loneliness—while tending a herd of sheep in the mountain wilderness—be explicitly explored on film.

In *An Unfinished Life* an added dimension is presented by the fact that both men are elderly; and it has been biologically demonstrated that older men tend to become more feminine in their behavior and physical appearance, when their testosterone levels diminish. Hallström chooses to show this idea in humorous terms by depicting Redford as a comic housewife and nurse in the early scenes, and later proving his underlying manliness when he attacks the abusive boyfriend.

Redford at his age can finally play the type of character he had shown affection for twenty years earlier, when he had made an old man, Amarante, the narrator of *The Milagro Beanfield War*. In that film the comic treatment of his quirky behavior, the thick glasses and the tottering steps, masked the inner wisdom of a man who believed in the ancient spiritualism of the Indian tradition and talked with the ghosts of his ancestors. This proves once again that there is a coherent line of thought and recurring themes that run through Redford's choices as actor, producer and director.

13. REDFORD'S CHOICES

Through line of a coherent career

After examining in detail a number of Redford films that deal with the American West and underlining his recurring preoccupations with the destruction of the natural environment and the plight of the American Indian, I would like to conclude by exploring how these themes are born out of Redford's experiences, how these works fit into his overall career as a filmmaker and how other choices of films that Redford directed, produced or starred in—from *The Candidate* (1972) and *All The President's Men* (1976) to *Quiz Show* (1994) and *The Legend of Bagger Vance* (2000)—are consistent with a larger interest in contemporary American politics and the function of media in society.

Redford explained his career choices this way: "I did so much work in the 1970's, that I wanted to stop for while, take a leave of absence to do some other things. There was a period of time where I did a lot of very diverse parts, beginning with *Jeremiah Johnson*, a film that was extremely difficult physically, made at my place in Utah, about a mountain man in the 1860's, a monosyllabic, uneducated character; the point was to show what happened when you brought the code of man against the laws of nature. Immediately behind that was a very diverse piece, *The Candidate*, a very urban sophisticated black comedy about the political process in our time; then came *The Great Gatsby* and *The Way We Were*, all back-to-back projects; then, during the time that I was making those films, I was preparing *All the President's Men*, which took me three years, as well as writing a book on an Outlaw Trail ride that I'd made, as a piece of Western history. So I had certainly been very active, but there were two things I wanted to do in the early 1980s, start the Sundance Institute and do political work in the environment, which I did; they both took longer than I thought, so I put out less product, because in between I was doing other things, but I did *The Natural, Out of Africa, The Milagro Beanfield War* and *Havana*. It was nothing other than that, I just chose to do something else for a while, and now I'm resuming my career more because the other's done; Sundance is doing well and I'm proud of it, the Film Festival speaks for itself every year, so I kind of accomplished what I set out to do, and I went back to my work."[1]

At the time Redford was talking about directing *A River Runs Through It*, a film very dear to his heart, and working as an actor in *Sneakers* (1992), which he called a piece of entertainment, but interested him because it was about privacy rights and the manipulation of information in a technologically sophisticated society. These statements confirm that he does see a through-line in his work, a logical progression among his various projects, the films, the Sundance Institute, and his political involvement; so it's instructive to review his perspective on his life and career as he explains it in his own words.

The American West

Robert Redford was born in the West (in Santa Monica, California, on August 18, 1937), when Los Angeles was still an unspoiled place where one could live in touch with nature, and it was the deterioration of his hometown into a dirty metropolis that spurred his interest in protecting the natural environment. "As a young kid, I loved Los Angeles. I thought it was a fabulous place, and I really believe it was. It was beautiful; I remember being able to see the mountains from miles away, and smelling fragrances in the air that you can't smell anymore. But L.A. was being poisoned, really, from the time World War Two ended. Los Angeles was our first victim of technology, our first warning of the environmental crisis."[2] He adds: "I watched green spaces turn into malls, the smell of orange blossoms turn into exhaust fumes."[3] This is why he decided to leave: "The air was going bad. The fruit groves were disappearing and giving way to malls and suburbs. Everybody just came and grabbed what they could grab and built what they could build. I took that personally. I wanted out of there."[4]

He had an eye-opening experience that he would never forget at age 11, when his mother took him to Yosemite as a reward for having survived a bout with polio. That is when he first realized how much he loved the unspoiled nature of the West and felt a need to protect it. "I grew up in a very cramped world, wanting to be out, in a different place. But when I went to Yosemite, I couldn't believe what I saw. I had never seen anything like that, couldn't even imagine it except in Maxfield Parrish storybooks. But there it was: this unbelievable view, this pure view that nature carved itself. And that began something that grew into what eventually became a very active concern for the environment."[5]

In the early 1960s he would find the ideal place to live—where he could raise his family in touch with nature—in the mountains of Utah: "I was exploring the West, tramping around a little bit, hitting the road, and I came to this place, and I remember saying to myself, I really want to build a house here, right here on this spot that I think it's the most beautiful spot I've seen so far."[6]

Redford considers the experience of building his own home a seminal moment in his life, when he felt that everything was falling into place. "I guess I'd always had strong feelings about the land, but they'd been dormant; now they were becoming explicit. And I could express them in building the house, working with my own hands, putting up a stone wall."[7] He adds: "Setting the stone framework of my house was one of the greatest experiences of my life. I felt at one with the elements of stone and forest around me and I still do when I'm here."[8] Those feelings of self-reliance in the wilderness are expressed in the joyous sequences of *Jeremiah Johnson*, when the mountain man builds a log cabin for himself and his family.

Redford believes that human beings feel spiritual nourishment when surrounded by the beauty of nature; he gave that kind of upbringing to his children and wants to leave the same legacy to his grandchildren. "I purchased some land in the mountains in Utah, and developed it in such a way that would leave them a legacy of the importance of having a piece of land, a space of your own where you could go to and invite your soul along. I do believe that, as time goes on, it's going to be more and more difficult for people to go to places where they can be quiet and invite a spiritual energy."[9]

In the 1990s, as a committed environmentalist and a liberal, Redford resented the way a conservative Republican president like Ronald Reagan tried to embody the western ideals by posing for photographs dressed up as a cowboy with a Stetson hat on his horse. He became interested in exploring the true values of the American West in his films, first with *A River Runs Through It* then with *The Horse Whisperer.* "We still seem to be so proud of it, at least judging by the way we mythologize western lore in advertisements, and by the politicians running around trying to act like western heroes, tough and stoic, independent and individualistic—none of which they are. So I was interested in exploring the truth of what that meant in a realistic, deep and meaningful way, not as this cartoon of family values that has become the electoral slogan of a Republican party bereft of ideas."[10] More recently he has felt insulted by George W. Bush's posturing as a Texas cowboy: "I take particular offense as a Westerner when I see all the swagger and all the strutting. It's synthetic. It's fake. What do they know about the West?"[11]

Redford, who has said, "My heart is in the West, I've spent a good deal of my life here," and "I'm happiest in the mountains and in the West," traces back his interest in the American West, not to movies or western literature but to his own life experience. "I became interested in the West before I read about the West, so my education and my interest stem from being in the West and seeing what I saw, from the time I was very, very small. I had already developed an interest about what was real in the West, so I just naturally followed that and it became a part of my life."[12] These are the books and authors that most influenced him: "I read about the West later in life, so authors like Vardis Fisher and (A.B.) Guthrie I read later; probably the first person that had an influence on me was really not in the West but the Midwest. It was Willa Cather, when I read *My Antonia*; then I read Laura Ingalls Wilder (*Little House on the Prairie*). That got me interested to read about the West."[13] He would use Vardis Fisher's novel *Mountain Man* as an inspiration for *Jeremiah Johnson* (Guthrie also wrote a novel about mountain men, *The Big Sky*, 1947).

Redford's interest in the American Indians also comes from personal experience, not from western movies seen as a child. "Now not so much, because somewhere along the line Hollywood Westerns became more real, but when I was a little kid they weren't; you know, Native Americans were never played by Native Americans, they were played by actors named Jeff Chandler, things like that. You saw that and you said, 'That's not real.' You'd go into the Indian reservations and you'd see what's real. So there was always a tremendous gap for me, and what I saw I had practically no interest in, because I had already developed an interest about what was real in the West. So I just naturally followed that and it became a part of my life."[14] He had felt a connection with Indian culture from an early age, while traveling to visit his maternal grandparents in Texas. "Every summer, beginning when I was 5, my mother would drive me down to Texas past all the reservations. In those days, the land was considered a wasteland. But I couldn't wait for summer to come. I can remember a tremendous connection with the land and the people. I always loved their land. As I got older, I was always rummaging around and exploring. I was always interested in the spiritual and cultural beliefs of the people. I was very taken with how they saw their land. Forty-five years of this involvement has really permeated my own beliefs."[15] He explains how his environmental involvement is born out of his respect for Native American culture: "I spent time on reservations in the 1960's, and then went into a really deep involvement all through the 1970's, producing documentaries, working with Indian leaders and feeling very akin to their way of viewing the world, especially as it relates to the environment."[16] He concludes: "About the only causes I'm passionate about are environment and the Indians. They go together."[17]

Environmental causes

Redford began his ecological involvement by fighting for local issues, such as opposing the building of a highway in Utah (1970) and the construction of a coal-fired power plant (1976) that would have raised pollution to dangerous levels; but he had to pay a high personal cost for his meddling in the state's economy. "When I started speaking out, on the issues that concerned me, the quality of life that we were going to lead, it bothered people. And, of course, if you're going to criticize an oil or gas company, you're going up against a million dollars worth of propaganda that they can use to brainwash the public, against you."[18] He later founded the Institute for Resource Management in 1983, as "a mechanism to deal with the issue of balance, of what we're going to preserve and what we're going to protect."[19] The IRM would put representatives of adversarial interests together to discuss mutually agreeable solutions to specific projects. For example, in 1984 IRM organized a meeting in Arizona between tribal leaders and industries trying to develop energy resources on Indian land, so that developers who wanted to drill for oil and gas, dig for coal and uranium on the reservations, could form an understanding of Navajo culture and their beliefs in an Earth mother; on the other hand, the tribes needed the revenue provided by mining and had to accept certain compromises. Redford says: "We recognize the fact that we are by nature a development-oriented society, but we must find a balance between industrial development and respect for spiritual development as well."[20] He adds: "My interest is certainly for environmental protection, but not at the cost of economic growth or development."[21]

Redford understands that America's westward expansion was founded on the idea of Manifest Destiny, theorized by historian Frederick Jackson Turner and President Theodore Roosevelt, as described by Slotkin: "The concept of pioneering as a defining national mission, the vision of the westward settlements as . . . a land of golden opportunity for enterprising individualists, and an inexhaustible reservoir of natural wealth on which a future of limitless prosperity could be based."[22] He realizes that to European settlers the American landscape seemed limitless, "Europe was already pretty well developed by the time we got here; in America we started a country that was barren and wild, lush and rich, so we had a whole different attitude about all these resources out here. They were to be conquered and taken and made for our benefit, and it was called Manifest Destiny, take whatever you can get in the interest of development. But now we're closer to the way Europe was then, we've got very little land to work with."[23]

Redford has the historical and literary background to know that warnings about the destruction of nature had been sounded before, by authors such as Alexis de Tocqueville, Henry David Thoreau, Ralph Waldo Emerson, Walt Whitman and John Muir; but in the last two decades the dangers have become more imminent. "Someone has always been there to warn us against what we were doing; and we were doing a hundred and fifty years ago what we're doing now, but now there's less of it to damage. It's all gotten so over-populated and shrunk that, when we do this damage, we feel the impact in a much greater way today than we did in Ralph Waldo Emerson's time. But unfortunately the people in power still aren't listening, so the struggle goes on."[24]

Redford has been involved in a number of environmental projects through the years. The Sundance Institute produced a 1989 documentary, *Yosemite: The Fate of Heaven* (the National Park that made such an impression on him as child). He is on the Board of Trustees of the Natural Resource Defense Council and declared in one fund-raising solicitation letter: "One of the main reasons I live in Utah is the immense expanse of wilderness preserved here by our federal government. These beautiful lands belong to all Americans—to preserve a legacy of pristine wilderness that is unique, inspiring and accessible to all of us." He solicited "citizens outrage" to stop Congress from selling off "our national treasures for the short-term profit of corporate interests." In the introduction to the 1991 children's book *Save the Earth*, Redford says that, after decades of involvement in the defense of the environment, it's time to find solutions. "Awareness is no longer the issue. Everywhere you go, you find that children know more about the environment than their parents. Like most people in my generation, I was brought up to believe in progress. We've poisoned the air, the water and the land. In our passion to control nature, things have gone out of control. Progress from now on has to mean something different. We're running out of resources and we're running out of time. What we are living with is the result of human choices and it can be changed by making better, wiser choices. Environmentalists now have everything we need for a grass-roots movement."[25]

Redford's proposals about the preservation of nature in the West are not conservative or nostalgic, but realistic. "Nostalgia is futile. I'm impatient with the armchair romantics who content themselves with the Ralph Lauren version of the Old West. And I'm impatient with a certain kind of idealism. It doesn't do any good to take the high moral ground with people who feel their livelihoods are at stake. They need a financial incentive. The African wildlife preservationists have arrived at the same conclusion. They have to give the farmers an incentive to protect the game, and tourism is that incentive. The same is true here of the wilderness."[26] He had deepened his interest in the preservation of wild animal life while shooting *Out Of Africa* (1986) directed by Sydney Pollack: "My interest in *Out Of Africa*—in the character I played and in the book—was the notion that we don't really own anything in nature, that we're only passing through."[27]

Redford's ideas are not based on traditional religions but on respect for the spirituality of nature. "I suppose I've gone through all the religions and rejected them, and in the end, this is what I come back to. The god of this landscape, of this nature, is the one who speaks to me. It's not a clear or even a hopeful message. Right now I'm on the fence about the future of the environment. Sometimes I'm an activist with a great sense of urgency, and sometimes I'm a fatalist who takes a very long and dark—a geological view of time. At those moments I remind myself that nothing is meant to last. These mountains will be worn down, that lake will evaporate like a drop of water; we'll probably extinguish ourselves as a species. The sediment at the bottom of the Grand Canyon is five hundred and seventy million years old. When I'm feeling the weight of my problems, I go down and take a look at it. It improves your perspective."[28]

Despite his doubts Redford has been publicly active in the defense of the environment, particularly during the twelve years of the Republican presidencies of Ronald Reagan and George Bush; then turned to grass roots organizing after the environmentalist Al Gore became Vice-President in 1992. He said, "The two Presidents that we had, Reagan and Bush, were absolute horrors for the environment. So therefore you had to go public to draw attention to the fact that they were really ripping off the American people. Now you have Gore who's a serious man about the environment; and I suspect he's going to bring a lot to the table publicly. So the work in the environment has to be done on the grass roots level, because it's not going to be easy to turn around the damage that's been done in the last twelve years; so it's going to have to happen with neighborhoods and communities, state and local governments, that's where the action is going to be. I think publicly and on the higher levels Clinton, reflecting Gore's attitude, will try to do what they can. In the 1980s that was impossible, because you had people up at the top, who had control of the money and the laws, literally salvaging the environment; so it was like guerrilla warfare, you had to go out and do both public and private work. I don't think it will be quite as necessary now."[29]

Redford has stepped up his public involvement in the last few years, after the Bush administration reversed the gains achieved during the Clinton years. For a long time he has been fighting against government proposals to drill for oil in Alaska, and particularly resents the reasons given for this need since 9/11. "I have had issues with that for several administrations, it's not exclusive to this one, but I do not agree with this current administration's policies on how it's dealing with our environment. I don't think it's fair to take the issue of the Alaskan Wildlife Refuge and say that we must drill for oil because of national security. I don't believe that's true and I have the right to speak out against that if it comes up."[30] He adds that the oil business is behind the arguments in favor of drilling, and wants to make the public aware of those secret dealings behind closed doors; this is why he has lobbied against that in Washington. "The current administration thinks we should drill into a very fragile part of our own oil reserves for something that I don't think is going to produce anything but destruction of that reserve. The facts that don't get to the public is that it's going to take ten years to get the oil to the market, and when it gets there, it's only going to satisfy 2% of our energy needs. So why would we go take a pristine wilderness that's a natural ecosystem that belongs to this country's heritage in a spiritual way, why would we cut into the heart of that? For what?"[31] He favors developing alternative forms of energy. "I think that we should explore all kinds of options right now, because the thing that everyone agrees on is that we are far too dependent on foreign oil, and on one country where there's a lot of stability problems. For me personally, there's so much we can do to help our own country's dependence by just reducing our needs for oil. If you take fuel economy, the cars that are in existence, and you improve the fuel efficiency to 40 miles per gallon, just doing that will reduce the need for so many barrels of oil. It would far surpass whatever we could get out of Alaska. So it doesn't make any sense until you realize who's sponsoring the need to drill for oil, and then you look at the relationship that we've had with our own oil industry for decades."[32]

Redford has taken concrete steps towards this goal by joining Senate Minority leader Harry Reid, at the Campaign for America's Future's "Take Back America" conference in Washington (June 2006), to encourage elected leaders to end our nation's addiction to oil. In an opinion piece on CNN. com (May 30, 2006) he supported a campaign called KicktheOilHabit.org;

their first step was to challenge oil companies to offer ethanol pumps at gas stations. He understands that this kind of change can only be accomplished by working from the ground up: "A grass-roots movement is gathering today to promote solutions, like renewable fuels, clean electricity, more efficient cars, and green buildings that use less energy."[33] Redford hosted a Sundance Summit on Global Warming (July 2005) attended by Al Gore and mayors of 46 U.S. cities from 28 states who agreed to reduce greenhouse emissions and voted to make this an annual event (30 mayors attended in November 2006). He said: "I'd like to see this gathering, as we did last year, as an example of real optimism."[34] He became directly involved in the 2006 mid-term elections by supporting candidates, such as Bill Nelson against Katherine Harris in Florida, in exchange for a promise to stop off-shore drilling, and by speaking out against Prop 90 in California. As a trustee of the environmental group Natural Resources Defense Council, he sent an email to its 172,000 members and left phone messages to Democratic voters saying that Prop 90 "would severely damage our efforts to protect California's air, land, water and coastline."

The American sports ethic

Another concern of Redford's that doesn't have to do specifically with the West, but is tied in with the American ethic, is the spirit of competition, the philosophy about winning or losing, in sports and in politics. He had been an athlete and felt he had inherited a false legacy about sports as a young man. "In high school I began to suspect the idea of team spirit, the attitude that it wasn't whether you won or lost but how you played the game. The only kick I got out of it, I realized, was if hit a home run."[35] Redford had played baseball (as a left-handed first base), football (as a quarterback) and tournament tennis in high school, and later began skiing, while studying at the University of Colorado; that sport, along with horse-back riding, became his passion after moving to Utah and building his own ski resort. Not coincidentally the first film he produced—and started shooting even before *Butch Cassidy and the Sundance Kid*—was about a champion skier, *Downhill Racer* (1969). He used the title but little else from the 1963 novel by Oakley Hall, *The Downhill Racers*.

Redford, who was also a race-car driver, explains: "I wanted to make a film that was pure and simple about a racer. I wanted this movie to be the portrait of an athlete, a certain kind of person in American society. I felt I knew the person because of my early life in sports. It only happened to be skiing because I was into it at the time and thought it was something very beautiful and visual that hadn't been dealt with in films before."[36] Redford formed his production company, Wildwood Enterprises, for this purpose and filmed the movie in Sundance, with footage his crew had stolen the year before at the Winter Olympics in Grenoble, where Jean-Claude Killy won three gold medals. He chose Michael Ritchie to direct the feature because he wanted a realistic and gritty style, in order to unmask certain stereotypes in American films. "It had annoyed me the way athletes had been portrayed in films. They were always clean-cut, middle-American types who came off the farms and had great wives behind them and great moms and dads. It was a Norman Rockwell depiction of America and that's not the way I saw it."[37] In *Downhill Racer* Redford plays a ruthless competitor, a self-absorbed loner, not a pleasant or sympathetic character. In the end, when he does win the medal that he had been striving so hard for his whole life, he realizes that his victory is meaningless: "The guy wins the race because the other guy falls, the media flock to him, but he realizes that the next time the other guy won't fall."[38] It's a moment similar to Sheriff Coop's realization at the end of *Tell Them Willie Boy is Here,* that he has won by default.

The first film that Redford produced marked the beginning of a consistent pattern in the filmmaker's choices, "I'm constantly wrestling with issues as a person, my feelings about America, about the environment, the system. And I believe in working out that struggle on film."[39] After many years as an actor for hire, he wanted to have more control over his work, like an artist does, and make films that dealt with his own life and experiences growing up in America.

Redford starred in another film about professional sports, *The Natural* (1984) directed by Barry Levinson from the 1952 novel by Bernard Malamud, where he not only played the title character, but was involved in the production and the editing. Roy Hobbs is a man who in his youth had the ambition of becoming "the best there ever was," better than Babe Ruth; but his baseball career had been derailed by a murderous woman. Later in life he comes back to the game and fulfills his dream, he even reunites with his childhood sweetheart and a son he didn't know he had, in a departure from the novel's tragic ending. "I had already done a fairly straightforward, documentary-like sports film in *Downhill Racer*, and because of all the tradition associated with baseball, I felt the way to do a baseball story was the way Malamud had gone about it—in an allegorical, mythological way."[40]

Like many American boys, Redford had felt a closeness with his father while playing ball: "Baseball was a strong connection between us, when we played catch his troubles seemed to go away."[41] His childhood idol was a baseball player: "I only had one real hero as a kid, Ted Williams. He hit a ball with such grace and ease, but also with great knowledge. Yet it never seemed to show. It just was. He also did not have much use for fanfare. I'm sure *The Natural* was in part tribute to that memory."[42] He would do a similar thing as a father, and decide to start playing golf again later in life to share that experience with his son, Jamie: "I hadn't played golf for thirty-two years until two years ago when my son, one of my kids, grew up and became a real avid golfer; so I decided well, I'll pick it back up again to play with him."[43]

A recurring theme in Redford's work as a director is the difficult relationship between fathers and sons, which he explored in *Ordinary People*, *A River Runs Through It* and *Quiz Show*; he also identifies with the emotional father-son connection in other films where the protagonist serves as a mentor or father figure for an adolescent boy, such as *Jeremiah Johnson*, *The Natural* and *The Legend of Bagger Vance*.

The moral of *Legend of Bagger Vance* is that sports should be played for their own sake, to gain a deeper sense of personal satisfaction. "Winning is a false god and it brings usually nothing but unhappiness. It feels good in the moment, but it's like cotton candy, it's gone shortly thereafter. So what is going to give you sustainability, continuity in your life, meaning peace, is if you play from your true self just for the sheer joy of playing; because that's the way he used to play when he was young and that's why he won."[44]

In a way even *A River Runs Through It* is a film about the grace of sports, because fly-fishing is another outdoor activity, like golf, that many people have taken up in droves in the last few years. "I have the same feeling about fly-fishing as I do skiing, when they're both done right. I think it puts you closer to nature than anything else I know. The experience of fly-fishing requires intelligence, because you must know the way of trout, the way water moves. Patience, so time becomes a factor. And skill."[45] In the same way Redford sees golf as a sport that is played in an outdoor environment, which is close to nature (even though golf courses are manufactured by men and waste a lot of water).

Redford says he likes using sports as metaphor, because it contains life lessons and the dramatic device of a contest, "and golf is the most interesting sport of all to deal with the issue of the self, because you're basically playing against yourself. The only other element is nature and then the odds of life."[46] That is why he chose to fully explore his ideas about sports and their connections with the human spirit in Legend of Bagger Vance (2000), a film that he directed from the 1995 novel by Steve Pressfield.

The Legend of Bagger Vance

Redford cast Matt Damon as a young look-alike for himself in The Legend of Bagger Vance, as he had done with Brad Pitt in A River Runs Through It, because he identified with the dilemma of a golden boy who loses his golf swing and only manages to make a comeback to playing the game a dozen years later; it's a similar theme to The Natural, where Roy Hobbs restarts his baseball career as a batter sixteen years after having lost his childhood gift for pitching with his golden left arm. Redford said he chose to make the golfer a younger man, and turn Bagger Vance (Will Smith) into a foxy young man rather than an old crusty guy, to give the film a high-spirited energy. In fact, he saw the figure of the mysterious caddie who comes out of nowhere as a "coyote trickster," a ghost not unlike Coyote Angel in The Milagro Beanfield War; except in that case he was an angel of death for the old Amarante, and in this film he's a guardian angel, a spiritual guide for the hero.

What most interested Redford about this story were its mythological implications as a classical hero's journey, as defined by Joseph Campbell in Hero of a Thousand Faces (1949). "Someone who's at the top of their game, or at a high moment in their life in some shining way, suddenly, through some event, falls into darkness, becomes disconnected from the self or the soul; and then it's about the journey back into the light and whether or not they make it."[47] He considers that kind of redemption a universal theme that most people can relate to, "that will have some relevance to their own personal lives," and that he has himself experienced with the deaths and illnesses in his own family. "There's been plenty of that in my life. But there's not any one of us that hasn't faced some adversity in our lives where we're tested in some way or another, our character, our belief, our personal strengths are tested; and that's eternal."[48]

In *Legend of Bagger Vance* the tragedy that causes the young hero to lose his faith in humanity is a shattering moment during World War I, when his company is massacred in the muddy trenches of the European front, and he feels guilty for having survived. The narrator, played by Jack Lemmon, comments: "Confused, broken and unable to face his return to a hero's welcome, Junuh just disappeared." Rannulph Junuh had been a promising golf champion since his teens, in his hometown of Savannah, Georgia. Matt Damon explains: "Junuh was the Golden Boy of Savannah, not only winning golf tournaments, but excelled at everything he did. He is used to everything coming easily until he goes off to war. When he finds himself failing in that life-and-death struggle, his idea of the world and how it works collapses. As a result he comes back pretty down and out. He's given up . . . until an opportunity presents itself."[49]

After missing for ten years, without sending any news to his beautiful fiancé Adele (Charlize Theron), Captain Junuh eventually comes back to town, but his time is now taken up with drinking and gambling; as he explains to the young boy, Hardy, who still has faith in him, he's trying to kill his brain cells, particularly the memory ones. Meanwhile the depression has started and Adele has problems of her own, her father has committed suicide when faced with financial ruin over a golf resort he had built but now sits empty; so she comes up with a brilliant idea, a world-class golf tournament to which she seductively cajoles the two biggest golf champions of the day into participating. However the city council insists that there has to be a Savannah born-and-bread golfer to uphold the local honor; and Adele actually takes her clothes off to convince her former lover to accept the offer, but then leaves insulted when the man cruelly accuses her of having done the same thing to convince the other golfers. Of course, he's still in love with her and she with him. She will later apologize, after he's played quite badly the first day of the tournament, for having caused him such public humiliation: "I'm sorry, but it's not my fault, you're the one to blame. The way you're playing, your supporters—every man, woman and child in Savannah—are so demoralized that they can barely hold down their lunches."

Junuh smiles at this remark and will play much better the next day, but this tells us that Adele, like Ruby in *The Milagro Beanfield War*, is concerned about her community. She's a privileged Southern Belle, determined to save her father's dream resort, but she also feels genuine sorrow for the pain of her people; she understands how important it would be for them to feel pride in themselves while in impoverished circumstances. That is why she wants the local hero to win the tournament, because she knows how much that would contribute to raising the spirit of her townsfolk. This is another example of how much Redford cares about portraying strong female characters in his films.

Bagger Vance explains to the young boy, when he wonders if Junuh could really win: "Yeah, inside each and everyone of us is our one true authentic swing. Something we was born with, something that's ours and ours alone. Something can't be taught to you or learned, something that's got to be remembered. Over time the world can rob us of that swing and get buried inside with all the would-haves, could-haves and should-haves. Some folks even forget what their swing was like." As Redford interprets it, finding you lost authentic swing can be equated with regaining one's soul, coming out of the darkness into the light—which is literally visualized in the end as a golf ball is shot from within the darkened forest into the blue sky. The slaying of the dragon in this mythical fable has to happen in a more spiritual way, not by attacking the opponent, but by quietly reflecting within yourself to regain your sense of harmony with nature. Redford says that what interested him was "the character's battle with himself, the idea of focus, concentration, center, the way an athlete gets into the zone."[50] Bagger Vance patiently explains this to Junuh—while the director contributes visually to the fairytale feeling of the moment with slow-motion shots of the green field, flocks of birds flying over the trees, a red sky at sunset: "There's a perfect shot out there trying to find each and everyone of us and all we got to do is get ourselves out of its way, let it choose us. You can't see that flag as some dragon you've got to slay, you've got to look with soft eyes, see the place where the tides and the seasons and the turning of the earth all come together and everything that is becomes one." It's the same concept that Redford expressed at the end of *The River Runs Through It*, when, as the narrator, he concludes, "Eventually all things merge into one, and the river runs through it." He recognizes that searching for harmony with nature is his life-long goal, the way to true happiness; and this inspires his environmental activism: "I suspect from a very subtle, more political aspect, nature is always going to be interesting to me, because I am an environmentalist and I think the role of nature is extremely important, and I hate to see it abused the way it currently is. So any time you can present nature in any kind of a thoughtful or positive way, I'll probably do it."[51]

Not unlike Paul in *A River Runs Through It*, who achieves a state of grace and becomes a work of art while fishing in harmony with the river and the trout, Junuh finds his authentic swing, as the ball flies effortlessly over the green field. And he does not die in the end like Paul, he doesn't have to give up his love like Tom in *Horse Whisperer*, he is able to be reunited and dance one more time with the woman he loves. Redford wants to present an optimistic view of the world with this film, as opposed to his previous directing efforts, because he feels that people need it at a time when the political leadership is not offering much hope. "I think that right now we're living in a pretty cynical time, where there's not a lot out there that's reflected in the entertainment business that you feel very good about; it seems that the drama is drawn from issues like violence and despair and a kind of bleak outlook on the world in general. I think that's because there's been a loss of moral leadership pretty well throughout, almost wherever you look you see leaders that are collapsing in scandal or assassination or violent overthrows. So I always think, why not do something that has a more positive, uplifting spirit to it, with a kind of spiritual energy? To me cynicism is the beginning of a kind of death of belief, and that is sad; so it's not a bad thing to put some good work out, because it will bring people up a little bit."[52] It seems that Redford has come out of the darkness that caused him disillusionment as a young man, into a more positive outlook on life.

Disillusionment about American ideals

Like many Americans raised in the patriotic post-war years, Redford experienced a sense of disillusionment as a young man, which for him happened in the 1950s, while for many others it was the Vietnam War in the 1960s that opened their eyes to the lie of their upbringing, the crack in the facade, the loss of ideals. Redford made this feeling the impetus for much of his work as an actor, producer and director. "If I went back, I would say that what probably spurred me was disappointment. Those old-fashioned legacies you get as a kid turn out to be myths. That made me angry. I think I found something in playing out disappointment that has sadness in it. The joy came from, now I can make a film about what it feels to be part of that charade. For me there was always dramatic material in a character being blind for a period of time and very much a part of things. And then something would happen and he would awaken to the fact that it wasn't as he was told."[53]

The first movie he directed, *Ordinary People* (1980), presented a typical upper-middle class, suburban American family that wasn't what it seemed. Redford said: "I had very strong feelings about the material and particularly one character, that I had seen all my life but never on film, that cannot get in touch with her feelings and needs to pretend that everything is okay when it's not, and the consequence of that on people around her."[54] He felt he had been surrounded by that kind of attitude growing up and it bothered him: "What I saw as a kid was Republican perfectionism; you strove to create a perfect appearance, a perfect situation."[55] And he wanted to expose what was behind the facade: "I resented the idea that everything was fine. But people behaved that way. That's very American to pretend that everything is fine, as if that was going to get you anywhere. I guess a lot of my work went into bursting that bubble."[56]

Redford always felt closer to the dark side hidden underneath the surface, and has expressed that very effectively in many films, such as *The Way We Were* and *Quiz Show*. "When I was young, very early on, I was rebellious as a kid, I was kind of on the wild side; but it had to do with being uneasy about what I was being told was the truth or the law. Something in me didn't quite trust that, and years later I found out that I was right not to trust it; and that went into my head, so then, when I began to create art or make films, I was driven by the idea of showing what was beneath, what appeared to be wrong with this picture."[57] He was able to put forth his ideas even in films he did not direct, particularly when he worked with his friend Sydney Pollack, as we have seen in the case of *The Way We Were*. "If that character who appeared to be perfect, to have everything going for him, were to have an underside that was dark or carry some either damage or flaw, that would be interesting; so we agreed to develop that dark side and his particular flaw or demon was that he appeared to be a person that things came easy to, but not his talent for writing. What was underneath was his fear that he wasn't really that good, that deep a writer; so he struggled with that on a private basis and there was a contrast between what he really felt about himself and the way he appeared to be."[58]

Redford has confessed feeling a sense of guilt after his mother Martha died in 1955 at age 41, because he had not had a chance to thank her for always being supportive and forgiving of her son's wild youthful behavior, while his father was demanding that he walk the straight and narrow; he felt that her dying so young was pretty unfair and that made him angry. Shortly after that he was asked to leave the University of Colorado, because his drinking was out of control, and he left to travel around Europe, where he continued drinking and experienced some dark and depressing moments. So he must have mined his own personal experiences when he depicted this kind of tortured psyche in the movies he directed. Junuh in *Legend of Bagger Vance* has to learn to forgive himself for having survived while his comrades died in the war, just like Conrad in *Ordinary People* has to realize that he shouldn't feel guilty for being alive, while his brother died in a boating accident. Maybe it's because he was stronger, the psychiatrist (Judd Hirsch) says, and able to hang on to the boat while his brother let go.

As a young man Redford loved the feeling of being an outsider, even an outlaw (when he stole things such as hubcaps because he felt that the people who owned them didn't deserve them, and spent a couple of nights in jail); that is why he would enjoy portraying those characters in films. "Being outside the mainstream is always more interesting. Not that I'm from there. I grew up in the mainstream, in that Republican community in Los Angeles. God, everything was fine, everything was hunky-dory. I did what everybody did, I played ball, I had a paper route, I told the truth. I also got into trouble because something felt not quite right about it. But you're too young and inexperienced to know what the hell is going on. You don't have any voice for that. It wasn't until I moved out of it, that's when the interest came to attack it. It becomes fuel, fodder for your work. In your work you play against the system, you play someone just outside. That's the essence for me, those characters struggling against a particular system, a system that controls our own independence, our right to be independent. The only character I ever played who tried to get completely away from the system was Jeremiah Johnson, and he couldn't. There are codes and rules wherever you go. An independent life? You find out it's impossible."[59]

His need for an independent life is what attracted Redford to the West, which has long been a symbol of that kind of freedom in American history. Lee Clark Mitchell explains: "The one aspect of the landscape celebrated consistently in the Western is the opportunity for renewal, for self-transformation, for release from constraints associated with an urbanized East. Whatever else the West may be, in whatever form it's represented, it always signals freedom to achieve some truer state of humanity."[60]

Like many American males of his generation, Redford grew up in a family where the father was angry and distant because he worked too hard at a frustrating job; young Redford resented the strict rules imposed upon his behavior and couldn't resist the temptation to rebel. Eventually he left college to travel to Europe and study painting, because he was "dreaming of Utrillo and Matisse and Braque."[61] He said that his mother's death when he was 18 relieved him of the obligation to stick around. Later on as an artist, an actor and a director, he became interested in the inability to express feelings inside a typical American family of the 1950s like his own, where you were told to toe the line and not make waves; he compares this Celtic, Scots-Irish ethic to the ethic of the West, where cowboys are taciturn and resilient and not many words are spoken. He embodied this kind of inarticulate western hero as the mountain man in *Jeremiah Johnson* and as the rebellious outlaw in *Butch Cassidy and the Sundance Kid*, then deepened his explorations of family dynamics in the films he directed, *Ordinary People* and *A River Runs Through It*.

On the other hand there was a positive outcome to the repression present in the Redford's household, the fact that his family expressed their feelings through storytelling, because that influenced him when he started directing films, as much as his art and acting background did. "I find a lot of value in storytelling, because in my family, the way I was raised, people didn't communicate too much about their feelings and you weren't given lectures about life; but you were told stories and in those stories were the lessons, the information and the knowledge you were supposed to get.

But you had to figure it out, to decode these stories. It was a way for me to learn about the world, so later on in my life storytelling became a very important issue for me in art; and having been a painter, which is obviously very important to me, and then being a performer, there was time when it all came together in my directing and that felt really good."[62]

Another source of Redford's disenchantment with America was the time he spent in Europe at an impressionable age. In 1956 he studied art in Paris, France then in Florence, Italy; the experiences he had during the course of that year-and-a-half gave him an outsider's perspective on his country. "For me when I lived in Europe as a young man trying to be an artist, I was hugely impacted by European thinking and style, history and tradition; and that probably, without knowing it, shaped a lot of how I went about my life afterwards. When I came back to America, I was hypercritical of American politics, because I had seen the view from abroad about my country, that I couldn't see when I was in it. I thought it was very valuable and smart to appreciate the importance of history and tradition; there's a kind of elegance to a very old history, while America is not that old. So I brought back with me my impressions of Europe and applied it to my life back in America; and I am sure that the films I've directed, particularly the first one (*Ordinary People*), was reflective of those feelings."[63]

This exposure to European culture is also what gave Redford an appreciation for a different kind of filmmaking, which influenced his own directing style. "My love for international films began probably in the late 1950's, when I first went to New York as a young actor and I would see films which I had not been able to see before that in Los Angeles; I was very taken with how powerful they were and how different from American films. Then living in Europe put me in closer touch with not only European films but European ways of thinking and style. But the real kicker was in the early to mid-sixties; when American films were very much about the youth culture, almost cartoonish and caricaturing the culture, I saw films like *Jules et Jim* by Truffaut, *8-1/2* by Fellini, *Last Year at Marienbad* and *La Guerre est Finie* by Alan Resnais, and those films really impacted me. Sometimes I'd see these films over and over again, because I thought they were so original and inventive, and they were taking such chances with camera."[64]

The film that had made the biggest impression on young Redford, when he saw it at age 11, was John Huston's *The Treasure of the Sierra Madre*

(1948): "I saw these Hollywood actors like Humphrey Bogart looking sweaty, dusty and grimy. And it made such an impact on me."[65]

Redford's desire to write, produce and direct, came out of a frustration about acting. "Actors have notoriously been considered to be children; playing roles, acting like something they aren't. If you have feelings and an intellect, and a point of view, you want to dispel that, so you push harder to gain credibility." So did his need to become involved in environmental causes, "I understand the need for causes, because acting isn't enough. You tend to feel that your profession isn't very significant, and you look for more meaning."[66]

Responsible journalism

In 1972, while promoting *The Candidate*, Redford began to hear journalists talk about Watergate and thought about making a film on the subject. He met with Bob Woodward and Carl Bernstein, the *Washington Post* journalists who broke the case, and told them he was interested in the relationship between them, the fact that one was a WASP and the other Jewish, and that both were inexperienced reporters, but "they had done something that precipitated one of the greatest investigations in our history."[67] Skeptical at first the reporters became convinced of Redford's serious intentions and gave him the film rights to the book they were writing, which was made into *All The President's Men* (1976) directed by Alan Pakula, written by William Goldman, starring Redford as Woodward and Dustin Hoffman as Bernstein.

Redford was interested in the inner working of the print news media, whose main function in society should be that of government watchdogs as part of a system of checks and balances. "What interests me is how the whole thing was uncovered through the persistence of investigative reporting, which seems to be a dying art in this country. I think there ought to be more of it. That kind of reporting is a terrifically important part of our democratic system, and I want to know why so many papers lay back on the facts, what kind of taboos existed, what a newspaperman has to do to get his story."[68] He found out that, as newspapermen are chasing history on the run, they gather information quickly and they can be sloppy, but they also tend to be honest. He said that Woodward and Bernstein "have given us one of the top suspense yarns of our generation, which nobody would believe if it weren't documented with facts."[69]

That is why Redford wanted the film of their book, *All The President's Men,* to have a semi-documentary feel, to maintain the credibility and accuracy of a true story, and he was pleased with the results: "To an extent that surprises me, the movie I wanted to make is right up there on the screen: a movie about the truth, and how close we came to losing the right to know it."[70] He believes the press did their job in this case and caused the fall of the Nixon administration: "I think we were heading for some kind of Orwellian nightmare, and that it was blown apart just before it went over the line."[71] It was a victory for the common man, "If anything has been learnt from Watergate, it's that citizen involvement can move mountains; but I certainly don't think that it's altered the political scene."[72]

Redford says that in 2005, when the film was re-released on DVD in a 30-year-anniversary edition, the political situation had become much worse. "If Nixon had had control of both houses, and the Supreme Court, I don't know if that stuff would have ever come out. You can go right down the line, there's about 15 issues as strong or as big as the Watergate break-in was that have come and died out. The administration is successful at denying, and if they get caught, they just bait-and-switch and create some other crisis. The Democrats, rather than using it as a beginning to make sure it didn't happen again, they went to sleep instead."[73] But the media are no longer performing their function: "That film was a testimony to the courage of journalists. But I feel very bad about the state of journalism today. It's a lot worse now. Hard news has slipped away. The media has been lazy and irresponsible, not taking the challenge of exposing leaders who are not telling the truth. All the emphasis is on entertainment and sports."[74]

As a movie star hunted by the media, Redford has a keen interest in the journalistic profession. He wanted to understand the nature of the beast and he did that with *All The President's Men,* where the *Washington Post* reporters are portrayed in a positive and heroic way; but he feels that the integrity and sense of responsibility of journalists has diminished through the years. However, he still believes in the important function of the press, as demonstrated by his character's journey in *Up Close and Personal* (1996), directed by Jon Avnet and written by Joan Didion and John Gregory

Dunne. In this Hollywood film, Redford plays a television news director in Miami who has lost his position as a White House correspondent for the network—where he used to be a Washington insider capable of asking tough question to George Bush about Noriega, and he covered important international events such as the terrorist attack against a Marine base in Lebanon. Eventually he rediscovers his true calling through the love of a woman, and returns to doing the kind of work that is most meaningful to him—which includes uncovering illegal Pentagon involvement with armed groups that were trying to prevent the return of the Panama Canal to Panama in 1999. In the end, he dies a victim of his commitment to his profession.

Quiz Show

The clearest expression of Redford's sense of disillusionment can be found in his fourth film as a director, *Quiz Show* (1994), written by Paul Attanasio about the quiz show scandals of the late 1950s. After directing films like *The Milagro Beanfield War* and *A River Runs Through It*, which were about a rural environment, Redford wanted to try his hand at an urban drama that reflected the vitality of life in a metropolitan city like New York, where he has consistently lived and worked since the late 1950s (dividing his time between his apartment in the city, his mountain retreat in Utah and his home in Napa Valley). It was at this time that the young Redford, like many other Americans, was shocked when a congressional investigation revealed that Charles Van Doren, a college professor from a respected family, had consented to be fed the answers to the questions posed to him during the quiz show Twenty-One, by producers whose goal was to make an entertaining program and deliver the audience that the network had promised to the advertisers. Redford saw this scandal as the beginning of an "erosion of trust" in institutions, "the first in a series of downward steps to the loss of our innocence,"[75] that continued with other disillusionment; he cited at the time John and Robert Kennedy's death, Martin Luther King's assassination, the Vietnam War, Watergate, the BCCI bank scandal, Iran-Contra, the Savings & Loan failure, the Clarence Thomas hearings, the O.J. Simpson trial. And he would surely add many more disillusionments today.

From a more cynical European perspective, that takes into consideration centuries of historical events, it is easy to see how this American attitude that sets a country's loss of innocence in the 1950s, because of the Quiz Show scandal or the McCarthy hearings, or in the 1960s because of the Vietnam War, or in the 1970s because of Watergate, is simply a personal coming-of-age realization for each young generation. You cannot call innocent a nation that was built on the extermination of the Native populations and whose heroic actions in World War II included dropping atomic bombs on Hiroshima and Nagasaki.

This is how Redford explains the disillusionment: "When the quiz show scandals hit, the Van Doren family was so illustrious—poets, educators, editors—so God Almighty. Almost from the time this happened, a shift occurred. I have a theory that Van Doren's collapse brought down with it the notion of academics as the people of the highest calling and that they never regained their place. In the meantime, the media, show business, and anyone who knows how to play off of them have steadily moved up."[76] He makes a distinction between the simpler social landscape of the 1950s and the media-dominated world of today: "Entertainment now has successfully come through all systems of information, and when the story of *Quiz Show* took place that wasn't the case. There were hard news on television, where facts were verified, it was pretty much the truth as we could understand it; then we moved to documentaries, which was the truth but filmed; third there were films that dramatized history, and films could take a certain amount of license, because it was dramatizing history, like Shakespeare dramatized history with *Julius Caesar*; and dramatists, film-makers and poets throughout time have been taking a certain license with history in order to make a dramatic piece. There was always a very clear difference between these three forms, now I don't think there is, because entertainment has gone through all the systems; and you can see it on television, you can see how news people now are trying to be entertaining, weathermen are entertaining; so clearly entertainment has finally made its mark all the way across our society."[77]

The investigator's disappointment is expressed at the end of the film, when representatives of the NBC Network and of the sponsor, Geritol, lie under oath and their companies are not indicted: "We thought we were going to get television, but television is going to get us."

Redford is aware that his ideas about the world didn't come from television, as they do for people of younger generations, but from books, from the times when he was taken to the library by his parents as a child and became fascinated with mythology. He also understands what it means to be in awe of the charmed life of an upper-class intellectual family like the Van Dorens; after all, he had played a man longing for the perfection of an aristocratic life in *The Great Gatsby* (1974) from the 1925 novel by F. Scott Fitzgerald. In *Quiz Show* the story is told from the point of view of Congressional investigator John Goodwin (Rob Morrow), a Harvard educated middle-class Jew who admires Van Doren and his family and is trying to keep him out of the scandal; so much so that his wife, who's the conscience of the piece, has to point out to him, "A quiz show investigation without Van Doren is like *Hamlet* without anyone playing Hamlet."

The morality of the situation is what interests Redford the most in *Quiz Show*. He admires the fact that Charles Van Doren (Ralph Fiennes) was still able to feel shame for what he had done and publicly admit his wrong-doing; although he inserts a senator's comment: "I don't believe an adult of your intelligence should be commended for simply, at long last, telling the truth." Van Doren's excuse was the same as that employed by the novelist who sells out to Hollywood in *The Way We Were*: "In a way he was like the country he lived in. Everything came too easily to him. But at least he knew it." Redford remembers that when he was growing up he could still be made ashamed of having behaved badly by his mother's reproachful remarks, and is afraid that in today's society we have lost all sense of shame.

Redford is right to believe that a sense of morality is still a useful tool in dealing with a changing world, and that it should not be forgotten; but his philosophy appears too Manicheistic. On one side there are the good values, literature and high culture, preservation of the environment, truth; on the other side the evil of television, the greed of real-estate developers and the merchant mentality of Hollywood films. Believing in such a clear-cut dichotomy between good and evil, truth and falsehood, runs the risk of turning Redford into a righteous moralist—"Saint Bob", as John Milius calls him. But at least he's somebody who has the courage of his convictions and he's not afraid to stand up for what he believes, as he has demonstrated more forcefully in the last few years, since the beginning of the Bush administration.

Political Commitment

The second film Robert Redford produced—*The Candidate* (1972) also directed by Michael Ritchie—was about electoral politics, and again about winning and losing, like *Downhill Racer* (1969). Although Redford looks a little like Robert Kennedy in the film, the director says it wasn't a Kennedy that they had in mind for the character, but somebody like Ralph Nader or Jerry Brown, who hates politics then gets involved in it. An idealistic young lawyer called Bill McKay, whose father had been governor of California (like Jerry Brown), is persuaded to run for the Senate by the Democratic party—although he has no hope of winning—with the promise that he will be able to talk about his progressive ideas. Surprisingly the public likes his honest approach and elects him, but during the campaign's process the candidate's beliefs have become empty words. Redford explains: "*The Candidate* was a film about what we do to get people elected in this country; rather than putting forth a position or an ideology having to do with issues, it's all about image and looks, on the assumption that finally this is what the country is most interested in."[78] He adds: "I mean, politics today is so much about lying, so much about deception, so much of it is contrived. A campaign is like a movie with all the image makers and everything."[79]

The film turned out so eerily similar to current events that in the summer of 1972 Redford took it on the same campaign trail as the presidential candidates, Richard Nixon and George McGovern, and drew bigger crowds. In those days Redford was hoping that a film such as this would get young people interested in the political process. "When we were releasing *The Candidate* in 1972, we thought we had a terrific film for young people, because that was when the 18-year-olds obtained the vote, so we tried to promote that awareness, 'Use that power!' And it didn't work at all, they didn't vote; so that puzzled me and I wondered why."[80] He understood later that the political process had become too corrupt for people to care: "Unfortunately nothing has changed there, the only difference is that it's become so low that there's virtually no buffer between what someone will do to affect his image and the truth. I'm absolutely fed up with electoral politics, it's so degraded; I believe the loss of individuality over the last few years, the emphasis on power and money, has taken away a sense of community; for me the community has a soul, therefore we have some kind of a disease of the soul, a sickness that has affected our politics. We have a political system that is so constipated that virtually cannot move, so much so that many people are leaving it, saying, look, I'm a human being, I have just so many years on this planet to do what I can do, so I'm not going to be in this system anymore, because it's practically dysfunctional, it's been manipulated by people who are only interested in control, without trying to do anything substantial."[81]

Redford has long believed that meaningful change can only come from the bottom up, from the people, "all the movement in our society comes out of the communities and the grass roots."[82] During a conference he organized in Denver about Clean Air Futures in 1988, he said: "I think what we see now is that the common will of the people seems to be stronger than the leadership or the will of the politicians."[83] He has continued his involvement in environmental causes along those lines, as we saw with his recent support of the Kick the Oil Habit campaign. "I don't work on a national level unless it's for the environment, which I continue to do; I do political work but it's on a lower level, I go and support people running for Congress, because I believe that the real changes that are going to occur in politics are going to be from the grass roots, they're going to come from the bottom up, not from the top, because the top is too much controlled by vested interest and business."[84]

Actually Redford personally helped Jimmy Carter with his presidential campaign in 1976, by showing up at his house with films of the Kennedy-Nixon debate to coach him on how to effectively debate his opponent on television, and he admires his contributions to this day: "His concern for peace, human rights and justice was more than evident when he was in office, but even more so after he left office."[85]

It is interesting to notice that, although in *Sneakers* (1992) he played a computer hacker with anti-government ideals developed during the 1960s, and became identified with the counter-culture after *Butch Cassidy and the Sundance Kid* (1969), Redford belongs to an older generation and was not politically involved in the anti-war movement of those years. "I was not part of any great movement in the sixties, I was busy raising a family with very young children, I was struggling to be an actor, I was concentrated on my career. I had as much anger and disdain as everybody did for what was going on, but I was not in the streets marching or burning anything."[86] He was an individualist. "As far as causes are concerned, I spent most of my life being anti-cause and certainly anti-group. I felt right off the bat, for example that the Vietnam War was a waste, but I assumed that the wars are drummed up by businessmen and government officials. And so I wouldn't even waste my time with it, and I tuned out on it in the early sixties because I just felt it was to no avail. I concentrated on acting. I just didn't trust the anti-war movement. I didn't think it was really going to amount to anything. And no matter how many people burnt their cards in Miami or marched with their placards in Washington, I thought it was just a waste of time. I was wrong, of course, but I really didn't get involved until I started getting caught up personally on specific issues that I could deal with and feel like I could have an impact. Invariably it turned out to be something smaller, like when they were putting in a road up a canyon in Utah. I react to things that make me personally angry or affect me personally. And there are certain causes that affect me personally."[87]

Redford's political consciousness, that would later push him to action in the 1970s, was born while he was in Europe. He said that he was living in a bohemian area of Paris where there were a lot of students, and when they challenged him politically, they let him know he didn't know anything about his own country's politics, he felt stupid; it was embarrassing and humiliating. So he began to read about US politics in foreign publications and came up with a very different point of view about the American political system than what he had grown up with in California, at a time when the governor, Earl Warren, and the State Senator, Richard Nixon, were both Republicans; so by the time he came back to Los Angeles he was pretty radicalized. He remembers a seminal moment, when he met refugees of the 1956 Hungarian revolution in Vienna. "I happened to be traveling from Paris to Rome to study art and I was staying at a youth hostel that was overflowing with refugees. And I didn't know what was going on, I was politically naive. I got involved in a conversation with a young refugee who had lost his mother and sister crossing the river. He said, 'You wouldn't understand because on American soil you've never been threatened to have your land removed from you. You don't know what that feels like.' And that was a pretty strong concept that had great impact on me, because he was right; so I went down to help the refugees come across."[88]

In the last few years, Redford has been critical of politicians of both parties, agreeing with Ralph Nader and Warren Beatty's assessment that

Democrats and Republicans have become almost undistinguishable. "I do think there's only one party, and that's because, when money controls the show, which it does in America, it's very likely there's not going to be much difference. The Republican Party in our country is really the party of money and the Democrats are supposed to be the party of people, but they've lost a lot of that because neither one wants to run the risk of losing an election. I mean, Clinton won by being so central that he managed to steal the Republican Party from itself."[89] That is why he believes that social and political change can only come from the bottom up: "It's down there, where the people live, that issues like education, the environment, children's health and so forth are going to come up; because parents and communities are going to drive then up. Nothing is going to change at the top." [90]

While always engaged and aware of political issues, Redford has become so exasperated lately with the blunders and lies of the Bush administration that he has been much more vocal in his fight against the government. He had supported the first reaction to the tragedy of September 11, the attack on Afghanistan, but opposed the unjustified war against Iraq. "I don't know in my lifetime that I've ever experienced a darker time in my country than now, because a lot of the fundamental principles that the United States Constitution and the Democratic process was built on are being threatened by the very people who should be representing them."[91] He identifies one of the problems of the Bush team as insular thinking, not connected to the rest of the world. "We are now led by a group of people that are extremely limited and arrogant and don't have any interest or knowledge of foreign cultures. I cannot imagine anything as extreme as going into war on an international stage without the support of our allies, because we are now a global community; so we can no longer be isolationists, separate ourselves out. I don't care how powerful we are, if we can't recognize that we belong to a union of other countries and other systems, then that's a terrible mistake."[92] He recognizes a pattern in this kind of wrong-headed policy. "I've lived through several wars, you know, I grew up during the Second World War here in Los Angeles; and I've experienced many threats to the American way, the democratic way: McCarthyism, Watergate—I made a film about Watergate—the Iran Contra scandal. So there have been enough scandals to kind of follow a pattern of what happens when one group has too much power and is too narrow in their thinking."[93]

Redford is particularly incensed about the Bush administration's abysmal record on environmental protection. "It's beyond criminal; not only is it a very mean-spirited policy by this administration, but it's really dumb to think that, for a short-term gain, short-term money advantages where you're supplying support to oil or gas companies, you're going to considerably destroy the health of young people, the air we breathe and the water we drink. If we don't balance between what we develop and what we preserve for our survival, we're going to be in big trouble; and there's no way that this administration is going to do it, they just have to be stopped and gotten rid of."[94]

He had withheld open criticism of the Bush administration at first, to show support for the government after 9/11. "The country was shocked by what happened and we all needed to pull together in solidarity to find a way to heal. It was a very moving thing that I witnessed, when we saw the strong lines between gender, race, class that used to separate us go away in a moment, as people reached out to help one another in compassion. I was very proud to be an American at that point. When this happened I felt that we all had a responsibility to put aside the voices of dissent and criticism, to commit our energies to pulling together; but the issues that existed that should be challenged, that deserved honest and open debate prior to September 11th, don't go away, they just get put on hold while we commit support to a government that needs it."[95] He had already been critical of the way Bush had claimed victory in 2000: "I was not proud to be an American during our election process. I thought that was a shame and an embarrassment, and there were some dangerous signs that began to appear that could threaten our democratic principles."[96] He has become increasingly disappointed after the 2004 election: "What sticks hardest with me is that this country, whatever concerns and doubts we had about the 2000 election—and there were many—were pushed aside to stand tall behind this guy. After 9-11, he asked for our trust and for our support. And he got it unconditionally. That trust has been savaged. The entire world gave him trust. And now look at what's happened to that trust."[97] And now he has declared that Bush should apologize to the American people: "Six years ago we held off, but considering what's happened, I think we're owed an apology."[98]

Redford has chosen a political documentary about the protests against the Vietnam War, *Chicago 10* by Brett Morgen, to open the 2007 Sundance

Film festival, because he believes that documentaries, "in light of what's happened in the past six years, have become more of a truth to power in an environment where lying is treated like a political asset."[99] And he is not afraid to claim his leftist credentials, "Anyone with a rational mind and a sense of decency is being positioned as a lefty by the extreme right. I believe in the tenets of democracy, and when they get pushed, it pisses me off. I'm left-handed. I'm not a very moderate person."[100]

His renewed commitment to political causes and his determination to question the aggressive foreign policy of the Bush administration, will be in evidence in the new film that he started directing in January 2007, *Lions for Lambs*, produced by Tom Cruise's new company at United Artists. Redford portrays an idealistic university professor attempting to inspire a privileged student in his class, who will later be one of two U.S. soldiers wounded in enemy territory in Afghanistan; Meryl Streep is an investigative journalist who questions a U.S. Congressman (Tom Cruise) about the truth of what's going on with this platoon stationed in Afghanistan. At least this is what was reported in the Hollywood trade papers. We haven't seen the film yet; but it looks like Redford will be exploring in a more explicit way tied to present-day realities some of his favorite themes: the responsibility of the press as watchdogs for politicians, the influence of a mentor on young men, and the revelation of what's beneath the facade, when a government lies about its motives.

In the end Redford is hopeful that the United States will regain their footing and learn how to feel connected to the rest of the world in new meaningful ways. "I guess I really am an optimist; I have no other choice. I do think we will bring ourselves back. We are a great country. I have great faith that in time the pendulum will swing. Things change. This is the time for new ways of thinking to take us into the future. The new voice and power will be social entrepreneurship. We cannot sit on antiquated ideas. We are all in this together. We are connected environmentally. We are connected on human rights. We have a responsibility on a human level to do whatever we can."[101]

CONCLUSION

I hope that this detailed examination of Robert Redford's career as a filmmaker, actor, director, producer, founder of the Sundance Institute, and environmental activist can offer insight into the way movies reflect and illustrate issues that are relevant and timely in our society. Redford at age seventy belongs to an older generation of American males who have traditionally dominated the cultural discourse and whose perspective on the world is being challenged by other points of views that were once on the margins and are now moving towards the center. In order to move forward it is important to understand and analyze the values and ideas of our immediate past, to see what needs to be saved as a legacy for future generations.

Redford represents and supports the best aspects of the American ethic that was formed on the frontier: the ideals of self-reliance in the wilderness, respect for the natural environment, understanding for the spiritual beliefs of the Native Americans, independence from codified behavior. He has been suspicious of the special interests that drive political campaigns, cautious about the influence of media and television, wary of the commercialism that drives the film industry. He advocates respect for the individuality of the artist's vision, attention to the truth, preservation of natural resources, the necessity of a moral stance.

A disillusionment with the patriotic ideals of the 1950s informed Redford's youthful rebellion that led him to drinking and traveling in Europe to study painting; there he developed his political consciousness and a perspective on America. He found an outlet for his tensions in his physicality—through sports and an outdoor lifestyle—he discovered a spiritual connection to the land and to nature that rooted his soul; he tempered his outlaw tendencies by becoming a family man and a responsible member of the community; he fought against indiscriminate development locally in Utah and nationally in Washington; he criticized a Republican administration that has reversed the progress made during the Clinton years.

As an actor Redford has embodied a series of flawed American heroes who questioned the world they lived in and he has produced and directed films that examine his country's ethics and the political process. He is an idealist but he's not naïve; he does not look with nostalgia to a beautiful past when the Indians were noble savages, he understands the reality of life on the reservation. He does not advocate absolute preservation, but a compromise between ecological and business interests. He supports independent filmmaking, but not in opposition to the Hollywood film industry; he's a player who knows the importance of entertainment, if a film has to appeal to an audience.

He has used all the tools in his possession as a filmmaker and movie star to express his ideas through films, making coherent and thoughtful choices throughout his career, proving that the art of cinema is an important means of communication in our society to discuss issues that should concern us all. He represents the moralistic values of an older generation, but he understands the new consciousness of a time where the information age and multimedia products are changing our way of interacting with the world.

NOTES

INTRODUCTION

[1] John H. Lenihan, *Showdown. Confronting Modern America in the Western Film.* Urbana: University of Illinois Press, 1980. p 4

[2] For theories on the director as the author of a film, see Francois Truffaut's 1954 essay in *Cahier du Cinema*, "On a Certain Tendency of the French Cinema," and Andrew Sarris essay in *Film Culture*, "Notes on the Auteur Theory in 1962." For the importance of the screenwriter as author, see Richard Corliss's 1970 essay "The Hollywood Screenwriter," where he specifically mentions Abraham Polonski's authorship of *Tell Them Willie Boy Is Here, Body and Soul* and *Force of Evil*. For the contribution of movie stars as authors, at least of their own performance style, roles and iconography, see Patrick McGilligan's study, *Cagney, the Actor as Auteur*.

1. TELL THEM WILLIE BOY IS HERE

[1] Lenihan, *Showdown*. 1980 p 22

[2] Lenihan, *Showdown*. 1980 p 57

[3] Elisa Leonelli, *Personal Interview with Abraham Polonsky*, 1995.

[4] Leonelli, *Polonsky*. 1995

[5] Leonelli, *Polonsky*. 1995

[6] James Spada, *The Films of Robert Redford*. Secaucus: Citadel, 1984. pp 130-131

[7] John Cawelti, *The Six Gun Mystique*. Ohio: Bowling Green State University Press, 1984. p 86

[8] Lenihan, *Showdown*. 1980 p 83

[9] John G. Cawelti. "Reflections on the New Western Films: The Jewish Cowboy, the Black Avenger, and the Return of the Vanishing American." *The Pretend*

    Indians. Images of Native Americans in the Movies. Iowa State University Press, 1980.

[10] Richard Slotkin, *Gunfighter Nation: The Myth of the Frontier in Twentieth Century America.* New York: Athenaeum, 1992. p 629

[11] Slotkin, *Gunfighter Nation.* 1992 p 629

[12] Robert Redford, *The Outlaw Trail: A Journey Through Time.* New York: Grosset & Dunlap, 1978. p 44

[13] Lenihan, *Showdown.* 1980 p 82

[14] Lenihan, *Showdown.* 1980 p 5

[15] James A. Sandos and Larry E. Burgess, *The Hunt for Willie Boy: Indian Hating and Popular Culture.* Norman: University of Oklahoma Press, 1994. p 3

[16] Leonelli, *Polonsky.* 1995

[17] Leonelli, *Polonsky.* 1995

[18] Leonelli, *Polonsky.* 1995

[19] Leonelli, *Polonsky.* 1995

[20] Leonelli, *Polonsky.* 1995

2. BUTCH CASSIDY AND THE SUNDANCE KID

[1] Lula Parker Betenson, *Butch Cassidy, My Brother.* Provo: Brigham Young University Press, 1975. pp XII-XIII

[2] *Butch Cassidy and the Sundance Kid* DVD. 20th Century Fox, 2006

[3] Robert Warshow. *The Immediate Experience: Movies, Comics, Theatre and Other Aspects of Popular Culture.* New York: Doubleday, 1962. p 138

[4] Warhsow. *The Immediate Experience.* 1962 p 139

[5] William Goldman, *Adventures in the Screen Trade: A Personal View of Hollywood and Screenwriting.* New York: Warner Books, 1984. p 464

[6] *Butch Cassidy and the Sundance Kid* DVD, 2006

[7] *Butch Cassidy and the Sundance Kid* DVD, 2006

[8] *Butch Cassidy and the Sundance Kid* DVD, 2006

[9] Molly Haskell, *From Reverence to Rape. The Treatment of Women in Movies.* University of Chicago Press, 1974. p 24

[10] *Butch Cassidy and the Sundance Kid* DVD, 2006

[11] *Butch Cassidy and the Sundance Kid* DVD, 2006

[12] Robert Ray, *A Certain Tendency of the Hollywood Cinema, 1930-1980.* Princeton: Princeton University Press, 1985. p 305

[13] *Butch Cassidy and the Sundance Kid* DVD, 2006

[14] *Butch Cassidy and the Sundance Kid* DVD, 2006

[15] *Butch Cassidy and the Sundance Kid* DVD, 2006

[16] *Butch Cassidy and the Sundance Kid* DVD, 2006

17   *Butch Cassidy and the Sundance Kid* DVD, 2006

18   *Movieline*, July 1997.

19   *Butch Cassidy and the Sundance Kid* DVD, 2006

20   *Butch Cassidy and the Sundance Kid* DVD, 2006

21   *Butch Cassidy and the Sundance Kid* DVD, 2006

22   *Butch Cassidy and the Sundance Kid* DVD, 2006

23   *Butch Cassidy and the Sundance Kid* DVD, 2006

24   Haskell, *From Reverence to Rape.* 1974 p 338

25   Cawelti,*The Six-Gun Mystique.* 1984 p 76

26   Eve Kosofsky Sedgwick, *Epistemology of the Closet.* Berkeley: University of California Press, 1990. p 15

27   Haskell, *From Reverence to Rape.* 1974 p 24

28   Haskell, *From Reverence to Rape.* 1974 p 24

29   Betenson. *Butch Cassidy, My Brother.* 1975 p IX

30   Michael Coyne, *The Crowded Prairie: American National Identity in the Hollywood Western.* New York, St Martin's Press, 1997. p 146

31   Cawelti, *The Six-Gun Mystique.* 1984 p 104

32   Cawelti, *The Six-Gun Mystique.* 1984 pp 106-107

33   Ray, *A Certain Tendency of the Hollywood Cinema.* 1985. pp 297, 299, 303, 304, 311, 312

3. THE OUTLAW TRAIL

1   *The Washington Post*, March 21, 1979. "From Butch Cassidy To the Sun Lobby Kid; Robert Redford Walks A Fine Line Between Issues and Autographs" by Lynn Darling

2   Robert Redford,*The Outlaw Trail.* New York: Grosset & Dunlap, 1978. p 17

3   Redford,*The Outlaw Trail.* 1978 p 12

4   Redford,*The Outlaw Trail.* 1978 p 153

5   Rita Parks, *The Western Hero in Film and Television. Mass Media Mythology.* AnnArbor: University of Michigan Research Press, 1982. p 53

6   Elisa Leonelli, *Original Interview with Lawrence Kasdan.* HFPA 1994

7   Redford, *The Outlaw Trail.* 1978 p 9

8   *Rocky Mountain Magazine*, 1979. "The other side of Robert Redford" by Michael Rogers

9   Redford,*The Outlaw Trail.* 1978 p 30

10   Redford,*The Outlaw Trail.* 1978 p 24

11   Redford,*The Outlaw Trail.* 1978 p 40

12   Redford,*The Outlaw Trail.* 1978 p 178

13   *Rocky Mountain Magazine*, 1979

4. JEREMIAH JOHNSON

[1] Jim Kitzes, *Horizons West: Anthony Mann, Budd Boetticher, Sam Peckinpah: Studies of Authorship within the Western.* London: British Film Institute, 1969. p 10

[2] Henry Nash Smith. *Virgin Land. The American West as Symbol and Myth.* Cambridge: Harvard University Press, 1950. p 83

[3] Nash Smith,*Virgin Land.* 1950 p 83

[4] Elisa Leonelli, *Original Interview with Robert Redford.* HFPA 1994

[5] Elisa Leonelli, *Personal Interview with Sydney Pollack.* 1997

[6] Elisa Leonelli, *Personal Interview with John Milius.* 1995

[7] Armando José Prats. *Invisible Natives. Myth & Identity in the American Western.* Ithaca, Cornell University Press, 2002. pp 191, 231

[8] Leonelli, *Pollack.* 1997

[9] *Esquire*, September 1992. "Robert Redford. Alone on the Range" by Philip Caputo

[10] Leonelli, *Milius.* 1995

[11] James Spada, *The Films of Robert Redford.* 1984 p 171

[12] Spada, *The Films of Robert Redford.* 1984 p 171

[13] Spada, *The Films of Robert Redford.* 1984 p 171

[14] Leonelli, *Pollack.* 1997

[15] Parks, *The Western Hero in Film and Television.* 1982 pp 12-13

[16] Lenihan, *Showdown.* 1980 pp 47, 54, 82

[17] Richard White. "Frederick Jackson Turner and Buffalo Bill." *The Frontier in American Culture*, Berkeley: University of California Press, 1994

[18] Patricia Nelson Limerick, "The Adventures of the Frontier in the Twentieth Century." *The Frontier in American Culture*, 1994. pp 54, 73

[19] Patricia Nelson Limerick, *The Legacy of Conquest. The Unbroken Past of the American West.* New York: Norton, 1987. p 21

[20] Patricia Nelson Limerick, *Trails: Toward a New Western History.* Lawrence: University Press of Kansas, 1991. p xi

[21] *The Missing* DVD. Sony 2003

[22] Prats, *Invisible Natives.* 2002 pp XV, XVII

[23] Leonelli, *Pollack.* 1997

[24] Leonelli, *Pollack.* 1997

[25] Parks, *The Western Hero in Film and Television.* 1982 p 57

[26] White, "Frederick Jackson Turner and Buffalo Bill." *The Frontier in American Culture.* 1994 p 21

[27] Leonelli, *Pollack.* 1997

[28] White, "Frederick Jackson Turner and Buffalo Bill." *The Frontier in American Culture.* 1994 p 25

[29] Parks, *The Western Hero in Film and Television.* 1982 p 37

[30] Leonelli, *Pollack.* 1997

5. THE ELECTRIC HORSEMAN

1   Lenihan, *Showdown* 1980. p 155
2   Cawelti, The *Six-Gun Mystique*. 1984 p 10
3   Leonelli, *Pollack*. 1997
4   Jane Tompkins, *West of Everything, The Inner Life of Westerns*, Oxford University Press, 1992. p 93
5   Leonelli, *Pollack*. 1997
6   Tompkins, *West of Everything*. 1992 p 81
7   *The Christian Science Monitor*, January 16, 1980. "Regaining a lost element of film" by David Sterritt.
8   *The Christian Science Monitor*, January 16, 1980
9   Leonelli, *Pollack*. 1997
10   *American Premiere*, August 1980. "Sydney Pollack" by Susan Royal
11   Parks,*The Western Hero in Film and Television*. 1982 p 31
12   Leonelli, *Pollack*. 1997
13   Parks, *The Western Hero in Film and Television*. 1982 p 75

6. REDFORD AND POLLACK

1   Patrick McGilligan, *Cagney. The Actor as Auteur*. London: Tantivity Press, 1975. p 197
2   McGilligan, *Cagney*. 1975 pp 198-199
3   *Rocky Mountain Magazine*, 1979
4   Spada, *The Films of Robert Redford*. 1984 p 168
5   Spada, *The Films of Robert Redford*. 1984 p 179
6   Spada, *The Films of Robert Redford*. 1984 p 182
7   *New York*, Dec 10, 1990. "Redford: Our Man in Havana Breaks his silence" by Neal Gabler.
8   Elisa Leonelli, *Original Interview with Sydney Pollack*. HFPA 1990
9   Elisa Leonelli, *Original Interview with Sydney Pollack*. HFPA 1993
10   Leonelli, *Pollack*. HFPA 1990
11   Leonelli, *Pollack*, HFPA 1993
12   Elisa Leonelli, *Original Interview with Robert Redford*. HFPA 2001
13   Spada, *The Films of Robert Redford*. 1984 p 260
14   Spada, *The Films of Robert Redford*. 1984 p 261

7. THE SUNDANCE INSTITUTE

1   Elisa Leonelli, *Original Interview with Robert Redford*. HFPA 2004
2   Elisa Leonelli, *Personal Interview with Robert Redford*. 1992

3   *Architectural Digest*, June 1993. "Robert Redford. The Politics and Pleasures of Managing a Western Landscape" by Judith Thurman

4   *Town & Country*, November 2002. "The Natural. For Robert Redford, Sundance—his mountain retreat in Utah—has become the production of a lifetime." by Pamela Fiori

5   *Newsday*, March 17, 1988. "In the Wilds of Utah" by Joseph Gelmis

6   *Town & Country*, November 2002

7   *Architectural Digest*, June 1993

8   *Town & Country*, November 2002

9   *Newsweek*, May 28,1984. "Robert Redford, an American All-Star" by David Ansen

10 *Newsweek*, May 28,1984

11 *New York Times*, October 23,1983. "Redford's Film Lab in the Rockies" by John Lombardi

12 *Arts Review*, Winter 1995. "Robert Redford" by Dodie Kazanjan

13 *Arts Review*, Winter 1995

14 *Arts Review*, Winter 1995

15 *Arts Review*, Winter 1995

16 Leonelli, *Redford*. HFPA 2004

17 *Arts Review*, Winter 1995

18 *New York Times*, October 23,1983

19 *New York Times*, October 23,1983

20 *Arts Review*, Winter 1995

21 Leonelli, *Redford*. HFPA 2004

22 Elisa Leonelli, *Original interview with Robert Redford*. HFPA 2000

23 *Interview*, January 1997. "Redford's resolve. Can Sundance help keep independent movies from going soft?" by Graham Fuller

24 *Entertainment Weekly*, February 2, 2007. "Shall We Sundance?" by Gregory Kirschling

25 *Associated Press*, February 23, 2006. "Robert Redford says a 'fever' has taken over Sundance" by Jake Coyle

26 *The Salt Lake Tribune*, January 22, 1997. "The Reel Truth: Redford Reflects on Films, Flubs of Sundance '97" by Sean Means

27 Leonelli, *Pollack*. 1997

28 *Interview*, January 1997

29 *Buzz*, Dec/Jan 1996. "The Real Sundance Kid" by Ross Johnson

30 Leonelli, *Redford*. 1998

31 *PR Newswire US*, November 8, 2006. "Robert Redford Announces Sundance Film Festival: Global Short Film Project for Mobile"

32 *TV Guide*, January 12, 2002. "The Sundance King" by Mary Murphy

33 *Hollywood Reporter*, January 18, 2007. "Dialogue: Geoffrey Gilmore"

34 *Los Angeles Times*, November 2, 2000. "The Way He Is and Always Was" by John Anderson

8. THE MILAGRO BEANFIELD WAR

[1] *Los Angeles Times*, October 19, 1986. "Redford's Late Harvest" by John Wilson

[2] *Los Angeles Times*, October 19, 1986

[3] *Los Angeles Times*, October 19, 1986

[4] The Milagro Beanfield War DVD. Universal 2005

[5] *The Milagro Beanfield War* DVD. 2005

[6] *Chicago Tribune*, Dec 23, 2004. "Robert Redford: a force for movies with passion for politics" by Michael Wilmington

[7] *Esquire*, September 1992. "Robert Redford. Alone on the Range" by Philip Caputo.

[8] *Los Angeles Times*, October 19, 1986

[9] *Los Angeles Times*, March 27, 1988. "Milagro Beanfield Grew for Producer Redford" by Charles Champlin

[10] *Los Angeles Times*, October 19, 1986

[11] *The Milagro Beanfield War* DVD. 2005

[12] *The Milagro Beanfield War* DVD. 2005

[13] Patricia Nelson Limerick, *Trails: Toward a New Western History*. 1991

[14] *Chicago Tribune*, June 14, 1995. "Dances with Disney; 'Pocahontas' is more than a movie to Russell Means" by Mike Kiley

[15] Warshow, *The Immediate Experience*. 1962 p 137

[16] Sandra Kay Schackel. "Women in Western Films: The Civilizer, the Salon Singer, and Their Modern Sisters." *Shooting Stars. Heroes and Heroines of Western Films*. Edited by Archie McDonald. Bloomington: Indiana University Press, 1987.

9. A RIVER RUNS THROUGH IT

[1] *Venice. Los Angeles Arts and Entertainment Magazine,* October 1992. "Above Politics. Director Robert Redford discusses family, religion, politics, fly-fishing, and A River Runs Through It" by Elisa Leonelli

[2] Leonelli, *Venice.* October 1992

[3] Leonelli, *Redford.* HFPA 2001

[4] Elisa Leonelli, *Personal Interview with Brad Pitt.* 1992

[5] Leonelli, *Venice.* October 1992

[6] Leonelli, *Venice.* October 1992

[7] Leonelli, *Venice.* October 1992

[8] Elisa Leonelli, *Original Interview with Robert Redford.* HFPA 1992

[9] Leonelli, *Redford.* 1992

[10] Leonelli, *Redford.* 1992

[11] Leonelli, *Redford.* HFPA 1992

12   Elisa Leonelli, *Original interview with Edward Zwick*. HFPA 1994
13   Elisa Leonelli, *Original interview with Brad Pitt*. HFPA 1994
14   Leonelli, *Zwick*. HFPA 1994
15   Leonelli, *Zwick*. HFPA 1994
16   Elisa Leonelli, *Personal Interview with Richard Friedenberg*. 1992
17   Elisa Leonelli, *Personal Interview with Emily Lloyd*. 1992
18   Leonelli, *Lloyd*. 1992
19   Leonelli, *Redford*. 1992
20   Robert Murray Davis, *Playing Cowboys. Low Culture and High Art in the Western*. Norman, University of Oklahoma Press, 1991. p 152
21   Murray Davis, *Playing Cowboys*. 1991 p xxiii
22   Cawelti, *The Six-Gun Mystique*. 1984 p 4

10. NATIVE AMERICANS

1   *Los Angeles Times*, July 22, 1990. "Searching for Chee" by John Wilson
2   *Rocky Mountain Magazine*, 1979
3   *Los Angeles Times*, August 19, 1990. "Lou Diamond Phillips: from Young Gun to Young Writer" by Kirk Honeycutt
4   *The New York Times*, May 14, 1989. "Navajo Cops on the Chase" by Alex Ward
5   *Star Tribune*, October 18, 1992. "Hillerman Country" by Jo Ann Shroyer
6   *Los Angeles Times*, August 19, 1990
7   *The New York Times*, May 14, 1989
8   Elisa Leonelli, *Personal Interview with Michael Mann*. 1992
9   Elisa Leonelli, *Original Interview with Bruce Beresford*. HFPA 1991
10   Leonelli, *Beresford*. HFPA 1991
11   Prats, *Invisible Natives*. 2002 pp 249-250
12   Elisa Leonelli, *Original Interview with Michael Apted*. HFPA 1992
13   *Maclean's*, July 27, 1992. "Verdict on Trial; Robert Redford reopens a disturbing case" by Brian Johnson
14   Leonelli, *Apted*. HFPA 1992
15   Leonelli, *Apted*. HFPA 1992
16   Leonelli, *Apted*. HFPA 1992
17   *Maclean's*, July 27, 1992
18   Leonelli, *Redford*. 1992
19   Leonelli, *Apted*. 1992
20   *Maclean's*, July 27, 1992
21   *Maclean's*, July 27, 1992

11. THE HORSE WHISPERER

[1] Coyne, *The Crowded Prairie*. 1997

[2] *The Horse Whisperer*, Production Notes. Touchstone 1998

[3] Elisa Leonelli, *Original interview with Robert Redford*. HFPA 1998

[4] *The Horse Whisperer*, Notes 1998

[5] Elisa Leonelli, *Personal interview with Richard LaGravenese*. 1998

[6] *The Horse Whisperer*, Notes 1998

[7] *The Horse Whisperer*, Notes 1998

[8] Elisa Leonelli, *Original interview with Kristin Scott Thomas*. HFPA 1998

[9] *Venice, Los Angeles Arts and Entertainment Magazine*, May 1998. "Scarlett Johansson - 13 Going on 30" by Elisa Leonelli

[10] Elisa Leonelli, *Personal Interview with Robert Redford*. 1998

[11] Leonelli, *Redford*. HFPA 1998

[12] Leonelli, *Redford*. HFPA 2004

[13] Leonelli, *Redford*. HFPA 2004

[14] Leonelli, *Redford*. 1998

[15] www.nicholasevans.com. FAQ

[16] Leonelli, *Redford*. 1998

[17] *The Horse Whisperer*, Notes 1998

[18] *Los Angeles Times*, September 27, 2005. "The Vaquero Way" by Jane Smiley

[19] *Canadian Business and Current Affairs*, November 21, 1994. "A kinder, gentler cowboy shows how: living legend Ray Hunt tames a wild Alberta stallion."

[20] *Spokesman Review*, July 13, 2002. "Horseman with a gift; Buck Brannaman, a real-life horse whisperer with local ties, shares his life story in new memoir" by Dan Webster.

[21] *The Arizona Republic*, March 31, 2006. "Original 'whisperer' shares horse sense; owners develop a relationship with their animal" by Kim Goetz.

[22] Leonelli, *Redford*. 1998

[23] Leonelli, *Redford*. HFPA 1998

[24] *The Horse Whisperer*, Notes 1998

[25] *Hidalgo* DVD. Buena Vista 2004

[26] *The Horse Whisperer*, Notes 1998

[27] Leonelli, *Redford*. HFPA 1998

[28] *Albuquerque Journal*, January 12, 1999, "Hi-Lo Country. Another Authentic New Mexico Portrait" by Larry Calloway

[29] Elisa Leonelli, *Original interview with Billy Bob Thornton*. HFPA 2000

[30] Elisa Leonelli, *Original interview with Matt Damon*. HFPA 2000

12. AN UNFINISHED LIFE

[1] *An Unfinished Life*. Production Notes, Miramax 2005
[2] *The Globe and Mail*, September 21, 2005. "Wrestling with the Hollywood beast; Robert Redford stars in just a handful of films these days. And his latest, An Unfinished Life, is becoming better known for its troubled trip to the screen than for the film itself. But Redford isn't letting it go" by James Adams
[3] *An Unfinished Life*, Notes 2005
[4] *CBS News*, September 9, 2005. "The Early Show"
[5] Leonelli, *Redford*. 1998
[6] Leonelli, *Redford*. HFPA 2001
[7] Leonelli, *Redford*. HFPA 2001
[8] Leonelli, *Redford*. HFPA 2001
[9] *The Salt Lake Tribune*. December 4, 2005. "Redford talks; about his life, movies, politics and Kennedy Center award; Redford on Hollywood, celebrity, politics, Bush, Sundance" by Sean P. Means
[10] *An Unfinished Life*, Notes 2005
[11] *An Unfinished Life*, Notes 2005
[12] *Sunday Express*, September 4, 2005, "Sundance battles on to the finish; Robert Redford's return to films brings him face-to-face with J-lo and a grizzly" by Pippa Smith and Andrea Perry
[13] *An Unfinished Life*, Notes 2005
[14] *NBC News Today*, September 7, 2005. "Morgan Freeman discusses his new movie, *An Unfinished Life*."
[15] *An Unfinished Life*, Notes 2005
[16] *Gold Coast Bulletin*, September 22, 2005. "Stars hope to ape *Baby* success," by Claudia Parsons.

13. REDFORD'S CHOICES

[1] Leonelli, *Redford*. 1992
[2] *Playboy*, December 1994. "Robert Redford. A candid conversation with Hollywood's most self-effacing superstar."
[3] *The Washington Post*, October 11, 1992. "Redford Crosses a Private River; in Montana, Making a Film from the Heart" by Toby Thompson
[4] *The Associated Press*, November 7, 1989. "Robert Redford Uses Star Status in Down-to-Earth Activism" by David Foster
[5] *Speaking Freely*, June 2, 2001. A Conversation with Robert Redford, by Ken Paulson, recorded in Nashville, Tennessee.
[6] *Playboy*, December 1994
[7] *Playboy*, December 1994

8   *The Saturday Evening Post*. 1978. "What Makes Robert Redford Run?" by Wendell Devidson.

9   Leonelli, *Redford*. HFPA 1992

10   Leonelli, *Venice*. October 1992

11   *The America's Intelligence Wire*, Sept 23, 2004. "Redford decries Bush's environmental policies in Vegas visit"

12   Leonelli, *Redford*. HFPA 1994

13   Leonelli, *Redford*, HFPA 1994

14   Leonelli, *Redford*, HFPA 1994

15   *The Associated Press*, June 5, 1992. "Star Watch. Star or Activist? The Two Sides of Robert Redford" by Dana Kennedy

16   *Maclean's*, July 27, 1992. "Verdict on Trial; Robert Redford reopens a disturbing case" by Brian Johnson.

17   *Newsweek*, February 4, 1974. "The Great Redford" by Charles Michener.

18   *Rocky Mountain Magazine*, 1979

19   *The Washington Post*, May 9, 1986. "The Capital Star System; Taylor and Redford in Town to Promote Their Causes" by Elizabeth Castor

20   *The New York Times*, June 25, 1984. "Indians and Industries meet to air Views on Land" by Iver Peterson

21   *The Washington Post*, May 9, 1986.

22   Slotkin, *Gunfifghter Nation*. 1992 p 30

23   Leonelli, *Redford*. HFPA 1992

24   Leonelli, *Redford*. HFPA 1992

25   Jonathon Porrit, *Save the Earth*. Atlanta: Turner Publishing, 1991

26   *Architectural Digest*, June 1993. "Robert Redford. The Politics and Pleasures of Managing a Western Landscape" by Judith Thurman

27   *Architectural Digest*, June 1993

28   *Architectural Digest*, June 1993

29   Leonelli, *Redford*. HFPA 1992

30   Leonelli, *Redford*. HFPA 2001

31   Leonelli, *Redford*. HFPA 2001

32   Leonelli, *Redford*. HFPA 2001

33   *CNN.com*, May 30, 2006. "Kicking the oil habit" by Robert Redford

34   *Deseret Morning News*, November 14, 2006. "Mayors hail global warming fight" by Doug Smeath

35   *Newsweek*, February 4, 1974

36   Spada, *The Films of Robert Redford*. 1984 p 122

37   Spada, *The Films of Robert Redford*. 1984 p 122

38   *Esquire*, September 1992. "Robert Redford. Alone on the Range" by Philip Caputo

39   *Newsweek*, February 4, 1974

40   *The New York Times*, May 6, 1984. "An All-Star Team Puts The Natural on Film" by Stephen Farber

41 *The Washington Post*, October 11, 1992
42 *Harper's Bazaar*, October 1992. "Weird wild and woolly; welcome to the offbeat world of Robert Redford" by Nicole Burdette
43 Leonelli, *Redford*. HFPA 2000
44 Leonelli, Redford. HFPA 2000
45 *The Sunday Telegraph*, January 31, 1993. "The Arts: last of the old-time cinema stars Robert Redford comes down from his Utah mountain and tells Sarah Gristwood about fishing, the environment and a long-awaited film."
46 Leonelli, *Redford*. HFPA 2000
47 Leonelli, *Redford*. HFPA 2000
48 Leonelli, *Redford*. HFPA 2000
49 *The Legend of Bagger Vance,* Production Notes. Dreamworks 2000
50 *Los Angeles Times*, November 2, 2000. "The Way He Is and Always Was" by John Anderson
51 *The Legend of Bagger Vance* DVD. Dreamworks 2000
52 Leonelli, *Redford*. HFPA 2000
53 *New York*, December 10, 1990. "Redford: Our Man in Havana Breaks his silence" by Neal Gabler
54 Leonelli, *Redford*. HFPA 2001
55 *New York*. December 10, 1990
56 *New York*. December 10, 1990
57 Leonelli, *Redford*. HFPA 2004
58 Leonelli, *Redford*. HFPA 2000
59 *Los Angeles Times*, December 9, 1990. "Down from the mountain; Robert Redford used to make his movies and take his chances, but now marketing goes with the territory. He doesn't like it much" by Hilary de Vries
60 Lee Clark Mitchell, *Westerns. Making the Man in Fiction and Films*. Chicago: University of Chicago Press, 1996
61 *The New Yorker*, May 1998. "Existential Cowboy" by Richard Rayner
62 Leonelli, *Redford*. HFPA 2000
63 Leonelli, *Redford*. HFPA 2004
64 Leonelli, *Redford*. HFPA 2004
65 *The Dallas Morning News*, May 7, 2005. At 67, Robert Redford tells it the way he is" by Philip Wuntch
66 *Rocky Mountain Magazine*, 1979
67 *Playgirl*, August 1976. "Robert Redford" by Steve Jacques.
68 *Playboy*, December 74
69 *Playboy*, December 74
70 Spada, *The Films of Robert Redford*. 1984 p 236
71 *Playboy*, December 74
72 *Playgirl*, August 1976
73 *Salt Lake Tribune*, June 17, 2005. "Key lessons not learned, Redford says; Watergate Revisited; Redford reflects on Watergate" by Sean P. Means

74 *The Dallas Morning News*, May 7, 2005.

75 *Interview*, September 1994. "Robert Redford" by Hal Rubenstein

76 *Interview*, September 1994

77 Leonelli, *Redford*. HFPA 1994

78 Leonelli, *Redford*. 1992

79 *Esquire*, March 1988. "All Redford wants to be is Paul Newman" by Mike Barnicle

80 Leonelli, *Redford*. 1992

81 Leonelli, *Redford*. 1992

82 Leonelli, *Redford*. 1992

83 *Esquire*, March 1988

84 Leonelli, *Redford*. HFPA 2000

85 *The America's Intelligence Wire*, Sept 6, 2004. "Former President Carter says he received debate coaching from Robert Redford."

86 Leonelli, Redford. 1992

87 *Playgirl*, August 1976

88 Leonelli, *Redford*. HFPA 2000

89 Leonelli, *Redford*. HFPA 2000

90 Leonelli, *Redford*. HFPA 2000

91 Leonelli, *Redford*. HFPA 2004

92 Leonelli, *Redford*. HFPA 2004

93 Leonelli, *Redford*. HFPA 2004

94 Leonelli, *Redford*. HFPA 2004

95 Leonelli, *Redford*. HFPA 2001

96 Leonelli, *Redford*. HFPA 2001

97 *Chicago Tribune*, Dec 23, 2004. "Robert Redford: a force for movies with passion for politics" by Michael Wilmington

98 *UPI*, January 19, 2007. "Redford: Bush owes U.S. apology."

99 *Hollywood Reporter*, January 19-21, 2007. "Redford lands opening left hook" by Gregg Goldstein

100 *Hollywood Reporter*, January 19-2, 2007

101 *Fresno Bee*, June 28, 2005, Tuesday. "Redford focuses on society's solutions" by Rick Bentley

BIBLIOGRAPHY

Bazin, Andre. "The Western, or the American Film per excellence," "The Evolution of the Western," "The Outlaw." *What is Cinema?* Vol 2. Berkeley: University of California Press, 1967.

Betenson, Lula Parker. *Butch Cassidy, My Brother*. Provo: Brigham Young University Press, 1975.

Brown, Dee. *The American West*. New York: Simon & Schuster, 1994.

Brown, Dee. *Bury My Heart at Wounded Knee. An Indian history of the American West*. New York: Holt, Reinhart & Winston, 1970

Buscombe, Edward. *The BFI Companion to the Western*. London: Da Capo Press, 1988.

Cawelti, John G. "Reflections on the New Western Films: The Jewish Cowboy, the Black Avenger, and the Return of the Vanishing American." *The Pretend Indians. Images of Native Americans in the Movies*. Iowa State University Press, 1980.

Cawelti, John G. *The Six-Gun Mystique*. Ohio: Bowling Green State University Press, 1984.

Cooper, James Fenimore. *The Last of The Mohicans*. 1826. New York: Penguin, 1980.

Coyne, Michael. *The Crowded Prairie: American National Identity in the Hollywood Western*. New York: St Martin's Press, 1997.

Davis, Robert Murray. *Playing Cowboys. Low Culture and High Art in the Western*. Norman: University of Oklahoma Press, 1991.

Ehrlich, Gretel. *The Solace of Open Spaces*. New York: Viking Penguin, 1985

Evans, Nicholas. *The Horse Whisperer*. New York: Delacorte Press, 1995.

Everson, William K. *The Hollywood Western*. Secaucus: Citadel, 1992.

Fenin, George, and William Everson. *The Western: from Silents to the Seventies*. New York: Grossman, 1973.

Fisher, Vardis. *Mountain Man: A Novel of Male and Female in the Early American West*. New York: Morrow, 1965.

Goldman, William. *Adventures in the Screen Trade: A Personal View of Hollywood and Screenwriting*. New York: Warner Books, 1984.

Haskell, Molly. *From Revenge to Rape: The Treatment of Women in Movies*. Chicago, Illinois: University of Chicago Press, 1974.

Hillerman, Tony. *The Dark Wind*. New York: Harper, 1982

Hitt, Jim. *The American West from Fiction (1823-1976) into Film (1909-1986)*. Jefferson: McFarland, 1990

Iverson, Peter. *When Indians Became Cowboys*. University of Oklahoma Press, 1994

Jordan, Theresa. *Riding the White Horse Home: A Western Family Album*. New York: Vintage Books, 1993

Kinder, Marsha. *Playing with Power. In Movies, Television, and Video games. From Muppet Babies to Teenage Mutant Ninja Turtles*. Berkeley: University of California Press, 1991.

Kitses, Jim. *Horizons West: Anthony Mann, Budd Boetticher, Sam Peckinpah: Studies of Authorship within the Western*. London: British Film Institute, 1969.

Lawton, Harry. *Willie Boy: A Desert Manhunt*. Balboa Island: Malki Museum Press, 1960

Lenihan, John H. *Showdown. Confronting Modern America in the Western Film.* Urbana: University of Illinois Press, 1980.

Limerick, Patricia Nelson. *The Legacy of Conquest: the Unbroken Past of the American West.* New York: Norton, 1987

Limerick, Patricia Nelson, *Trails: Towards a New Western History.* Edited by Patricia Nelson Limerick, Clyde A.Milner II, Charles E. Rankin. Lawrence: University Press of Kansas, 1991

Maclean, Norman. *A River Runs Through It, and other stories.* Chicago: University of Chicago Press, 1976

McGilligan, Patrick. *Cagney. The Actor As Auteur.* London: Tantivity Press, 1975

McRobbie, Angela. *Postmodernism and Popular Culture.* London: Routledge, 1994

Matthiesen, Peter. *In the Spirit of Crazy Horse.* Viking 1983.

Mellen, Joan. *Big Bad Wolves: Masculinity in the American Film.* London: Elm Tree Books, 1978

Nichols, John. *The Milagro Beanfield War.* 1974. New York: Ballantine Books, 1976.

Parks, Rita. *The Western Hero in Film and Television. Mass Media Mythology.* AnnArbor, Michigan: UMI Research Press, 1982.

Pointer, Larry. *In Search of Butch Cassidy.* Norman: University of Oklahoma Press, 1977.

Porrit, Jonathon. *Save the Earth.* Turner Publishing, Atlanta, 1991.

Prats, Armando José, *Invisible Natives. Myth & Identity in the American Western.* Ithaca: Cornell University Press, 2002.

Ray, Robert. *A Certain Tendency of the Hollywood Cinema, 1930-1980.* Princeton: Princeton University Press, 1985.

Redford, Robert. *The Outlaw Trail: A Journey Through Time.* Photography by Jonathan Blair. New York: Grosset & Dunlap, 1978.

Sandos, James A., and Larry E. Burgess. *The Hunt for Willie Boy: Indian Hating and Popular Culture*. Norman: University of Oklahoma Press, 1994

Schackel, Sandra Kay. "Women in Western Films: The Civilizer, the Saloon Singer, and Their Modern Sister." *Shooting Stars. Heroes and Heroines of Western Film*. Edited by Archie P. McDonald. Bloomington: Indiana University Press, 1987.

Sedgwick, Eve Kosofsky. *Between Men: English Literature and Male Homosocial Desire*. New York: Columbia University Press, 1985

Sedgwick, Eve Kosofsky. *Epistemology of the Closet*. Berkeley: University of California Press, 1990.

Slotkin, Richard. *Gunfighter Nation: The Myth of the Frontier in Twentieth Century America*. New York: Athenaeum, 1992

Slotkin, Richard. *Regeneration Through Violence. The mythology of the American Frontier*. Middletown: Wesleyan University Press, 1973

Smith, Henry Nash. *Virgin Land. The American West as Symbol and Myth*. Cambridge: Harvard University Press, 1950.

Spada, James. *The Films of Robert Redford*. Secaucus: Citadel, 1984.

Spragg, Mark. *An Unfinished Life*. New York: Alfred A. Knopf, 2004

Tompkins, Jane. *West of Everything: The inner life of Westerns*. New York: Oxford University Press, 1992

Tuska, John. *The American West in Film: Critical approaches to the Western*. Lincoln: University of Nebraska Press, 1985

Warshow, Robert. *The Immediate Experience: Movies, Comics, Theatre and Other Aspects of Popular Culture*. New York: Doubleday, 1962

Wister, Owen. *The Virginian: A Horseman of the Plains*. 1902. New York: Penguin, 1988.

White, Richard, and Patricia Nelson Limerick. *The Frontier in American Culture*. Berkeley: University of California Press, 1994

Wright, Will. *Six Guns and Society*. Berkeley: University of California Press, 1975

FILMOGRAPHY

All the Pretty Horses. Director-Screenplay: Billy Bob Thornton. Novel: Cormac McCarthy. Cast: Matt Damon, Henry Thomas, Lucas Black, Penelope Cruz, Rubén Blades, Bruce Dern, Sam Shepard, Robert Patrick, Miriam Colon. Miramax 2000

All The President's Men. Director: Alan Pakula. Producer: Robert Redford. Screenplay: William Goldman. Book: Carl Bernstein and Bob Woodward. Cast: Robert Redford, Dustin Hoffman. Warner Bros, 1976

Apache. Director: Robert Aldrich. Screenplay: James R.Webb. Novel: Paul Wellman. Cast: Burt Lancaster, Jean Peters, Charles Brosnon. United Artists, 1954

Bad Girls. Director: Jonathan Kaplan. Cast: Madeleine Stowe, Andie MacDowell, Mary Stuart Masterson, Drew Barrymore. 20th Century Fox, 1994

The Ballad of Little Joe. Director-Screenplay: Maggie Greenwald. Cast: Suzy Amis. Fine Line, 1994

Barefoot in the Park. Director: Gene Sacks. Screenplay-play: Neil Simon. Cast: Robert Redford, Jane Fonda. Paramount, 1967

The Big Sky. Director: Howard Hawks. Screenplay: Dudley Nichols. Novel: A.B. Guthrie. Cast: Kirk Douglas, Dewey Martin, Elizabeth Threat, Will Geer. RKO, 1952

Black Robe. Director: Bruce Beresford. Screenplay-Novel: Brian Moore. Cast: Lothaire Bluteau, Aden Young, Sandrine Holt, August Schellenerg, Tantoo Cardinal. Samuel Goldwyn, 1991

Bonnie and Clyde. Director: Arthur Penn. Screenplay: David Newman, Robert Benton. Cast: Warren Beatty, Faye Dunaway, Gene Hackman. Warner Bros, 1967

Brokeback Mountain. Director: Ang Lee. Screenplay: Larry McMurtry, Diana Ossana. Short story: E. Annie Proulx. Cast: Heath Ledger, Jake Gyllenhaal, Michelle Williams, Anne Hathaway, Randy Quaid. Universal 2005

Broken Arrow. Director: Delmer Daves. Screenplay: Michael Blankfort. Novel *Blood Brother*. Tom Jeffords. Cast: James Stewart, Jeff Chandler, Debra Paget. 20th Century Fox, 1950

Brubaker. Director: Stuart Rosenberg. Screenplay: W.D. Richter. Cast: Robert Redford, Yaphet Kotto, Jane Alexander. 20th Century Fox, 1979

Butch Cassidy and the Sundance Kid. Director: George Roy Hill. Screenplay: William Goldman. Cinematography: Conrad Hall. Cast: Paul Newman, Robert Redford, Katharine Ross. 20th Century Fox, 1969.

The Candidate. Director: Michael Richtie. Producer: Robert Redford. Screenplay: Jeremy Larner. Cast: Robert Redford, Peter Boyle. Warner Bros, 1972.

Charlotte's Web. Director: Gary Winick. Novel: E B White. Cast: Dakota Fanning. Paramount, 2006

Cheyenne Autumn. Director: John Ford. Cast: Richard Widmark, Carroll Baker, Karl Malden, Dolores Del Rio, Sal Mineo, Edward G. Robinson, Ricardo Montalban, James Stewart. Warner Bros, 1964.

The Clearing. Director: Pieter Jan Brugge. Cast: Robert Redford, Willem Dafoe, Helen Mirren. Fox Searchlight, 2004.

Dances with Wolves. Director: Kevin Costner. Screenplay: Michael Blake. Cast: Kevin Costner, Mary McDonnell, Graham Greene, Tantoo Cardinal. Orion, 1990.

The Dark Wind. Director: Errol Morris. Producer: Robert Redford. Screenplay: Neal Jimenez, Eric Bergren. Novel: Tony Hillerman. Cast: Lou Diamond Phillips, Fred Ward. Carolco, 1990.

The Downhill Racer. Director: Michael Richtie. Producer: Robert Redford. Screenplay: James Salter. Novel: Oakley Hall. Cast: Robert Redford, Gene Hackman, Camilla Sparv. Paramount, 1969.

Down in the Valley. Director: David Jacobson. Cast: Edward Norton, Evan Rachel Wood, Rory Culkin, David Morse. ThinkFilm, 2006

The Electric Horseman. Director: Sydney Pollack. Producer: Robert Redford. Screenplay: Robert Garland. Cast: Robert Redford, Jane Fonda, Valerie Perrine, Willie Nelson. Columbia, 1979.

Geronimo: An American Legend. Director: Walter Hill. Screenplay: John Milius. Cast: Wes Study, Jason Patric, Robert Duvall, Gene Hackman. Columbia, 1994.

The Great Gatsby. Director: Jack Clayton. Screenplay: Francis Coppola. Novel: F. Scott Fitzgerald. Cast: Robert Redford, Mia Farrow, Bruce Dern. Paramount, 1974.

Gunga Din. Director: George Stevens. Poem: Rudyard Kipling. Cast: Cary Grant. RKO, 1939

Havana. Director: Sydney Pollack. Screenplay: Judith Rascoe, David Rayfiel. Cast: Robert Redford, Lena Olin, Raul Julia, Alan Arkin, Tomas Milian. Universal, 1990.

Heaven's Gate. Director-Screenplay: Michael Cimino. Cast: Kris Kristofferson, Christopher Walken, Isabelle Huppert, Mickey Rourke. MGM, 1981

High Noon. Director: Fred Zinnemann. Screenplay: Carl Foreman. Cast: Gary Cooper, Grace Kelly, Lloyd Bridges. Republic, 1952.

The Hi-Lo Country. Director: Stephen Frears. Screenplay: Walon Green. Novel: Max Evans. Cast: Billy Crudup, Woody Harrelson, Patricia Arquette, Penelope Cruz. Gramercy, 1999.

Hidalgo. Director: Joe Johnston. Screenplay: John Fusco. Cast: Viggo Mortensen, Omar Sharif, Zuleika Robinson. Touchstone, 2004

Hombre. Director: Martin Ritt. Story: Elmore Leonard. Cast: Paul Newman, Frederich March, Diane Cilento, Martin Balsam. 20th Century Fox, 1966

Hondo. Director: John Farrow. Screenplay: James Edward Grant. Story: Louis L'Amour. Cast: John Wayne, Geraldine Page. Warner Bros, 1953.

The Horse Whisperer. Director-Producer: Robert Redford. Screenplay: Eric Roth, Richard LaGravanese. Novel: Nicholas Evans. Cinematography: Robert Richardson.

Cast: Robert Redford, Kristin Scott Thomas, Scarlett Johannson, Sam Neill, Chris Cooper, Dianne Wiest. Touchstone, 1998.

Hud. Director: Martin Ritt. Novel *Horseman, Pass By*: Larry McMurtry. Cast: Paul Newman, Melvyn Douglas, Patricia Neal. Paramount, 1963.

Incident at Oglala. Director: Michael Apted. Narrator-Producer: Robert Redford. Wildwood, 1992.

Indecent Proposal. Director: Adrian Lyne. Screenplay: Amy Holden Jones. Cast: Robert Redford, Demi Moore, Woody Harrelson. Paramount, 1992.

It Happened One Night. Director: Frank Capra. Screenplay: Robert Riskin. Cast: Clark Gable, Claudette Colbert. Columbia, 1934.

Jeremiah Johnson. Director: Sydney Pollack. Screenplay: John Milius, Edward Anhalt. Novel *Mountain Man*: Vardis Fisher. Story: Raymond W. Thorp and Robert Bunker. Cast: Robert Redford. Warner Bros, 1972.

The Last Castle. Director: Rod Lurie. Cast: Robert Redford, James Gandolfini, Mark Ruffalo. DreamWorks, 2001.

The Last of The Mohicans. Director-Screenplay: Michael Mann. Novel: James Fenimore Cooper. 1936 screenplay: Philip Dunne. Cast: Daniel Day Lewis, Russell Means, Madeleine Stowe, Wes Studi. 20th Century Fox, 1992.

The Left-Handed Gun. Director: Arthur Penn. Cast: Paul Newman. Warner Bros, 1962.

The Legend of Bagger Vance. Director-Producer: Robert Redford. Screenplay: Jeremy Leven. Novel: Steven Pressfield. Cinematography: Michael Ballhaus. Cast: Matt Damon, Will Smith, Charlize Theron. Dreamworks, 2000

Legends of the Fall. Director: Edward Zwick. Screenplay: Susan Shilliday, Bill Wittliff. Novella: Jim Harrison. Cast: Brad Pitt, Anthony Hopkins, Aidan Quinn, Julia Ormond, Henry Thomas, Gordon Tootoosis, Tantoo Cardinal. Tristar, 1994.

Little Big Man. Director: Arthur Penn. Screenplay: Calder Willingham. Novel: Thomas Berger. Cast: Dustin Hoffman, Faye Dunaway, Chief Dan George. 20th Century Fox, 1970.

Lonely Are the Brave. Director: David Miller. Novel *Brave Cowboy*: Edward Abbey. Cast: Kirk Douglas, Walter Matthau, Gena Rowlands. MCA, 1962.

McCabe and Mrs. Miller. Director-Screenplay: Robert Altman. Novel: Edmund Naughton. Cast: Warren Beatty, Julie Christie. Warner Bros, 1971

A Man Called Horse. Director: Elliot Silverstein. Screenplay: Jack DeWitt. Cast: Richard Harris. 20th Century Fox, 1970

The Man Who Shot Liberty Valance. Director: John Ford. Story: Dorothy Johnson. Cast: James Stewart, John Wayne, Vera Miles, Lee Marvin. Paramount, 1962.

Maverick. Director: Richard Donner. Screenplay: William Goldman. Cast: Mel Gibson, James Garner, Jodie Foster. Warner Bros, 1994

The Milagro Beanfield War. Director-Producer: Robert Redford. Screenplay: David Ward, John Nichols. Novel: John Nichols. Cast: Ruben Blades, Sonia Braga, Melanie Griffith, John Heard, Christopher Walken. Universal, 1988.

The Misfits. Director: John Huston. Screenplay: Arthur Miller. Cast: Clark Gable, Marilyn Monroe, Montgomery Clift. United Artists, 1961.

The Missing. Director: Ron Howard. Screenplay: Akiva Goldsman, Ken Kaufman. Novel *The Last Ride*: Tom Eidson. Cast: Cate Blanchett, Tommy Lee Jones, Evan Rachel Wood, Jenna Boyd. Columbia, 2004

The Motorcycle Diaries. Director: Walter Salles. Producer: Robert Redford. Screenplay: Jose Rivera. Book: Ernesto Che Guevara. Cast: Gael Garcia Bernal, Rodrigo De La Serna, Mia Maestro. Focus, 2004

Mr. Deeds Goes to Town. Director: Frank Capra. Screenplay: Robert Riskin. Cast: Gary Cooper, Jean Arthur. Columbia, 1936

My Darling Clementine. Director: John Ford. Book *Wyatt Earp, Frontier Marshal*: Stuart Lake. Cast: Henry Fonda, Linda Darnell, Victor Mature.
20th Century Fox, 1946.

The Natural. Director: Barry Levinson. Screenplay: Roger Towne, Philip Dusenberry. Novel: Bernard Malamud. Cast: Robert Redford, Wilford Brimley, Glenn Close, Robert Duvall, Kim Basinger. Columbia, 1984.

The New World. Director-Screenplay: Terrence Malick. Cast: Colin Farrell, Q'orianka Kilcher, Christian Bale, Christopher Plummer, August Schellenberg, Wes Studi. New Line, 2005

Open Range. Director: Kevin Costner. Screenplay: Craig Storper. Novel *The Open Range Men*: Lauran Paine. Cast: Kevin Costner, Robert Duvall, Annette Bening, Diego Luna, Michael Gambon. Touchstone 2003

Ordinary People. Director-Producer: Robert Redford. Screenplay: Alvin Sergeant. Novel: Judith Guest. Cinematography: John Bailey. Cast: Donald Sutherland, Mary Tyler Moore, Timothy Hutton, Judd Hirsch. Paramount, 1980

Out of Africa. Director: Sydney Pollack. Screenplay: Kurt Luedtke. Cast: Meryl Streep, Robert Redford, Klaus Maria Brandauer. Universal, 1985

The Outlaw Josey Wales. Director: Clint Eastwood. Screenplay: Phil Kaufman, Sonia Chernus. Cast: Clint Eastwood, Chief Dan George, Sandra Locke. Warner Bros, 1976

Pale Rider. Director: Clint Eastwood. Screenplay: Michael Butler, Dennis Shryac. Cast: Clint Eastwood, Michael Moriarty. Warner Bros, 1985

Pocahontas. Director: Mike Gabriel, Eric Goldberg. Disney, 1995

Posse. Director: Mario Van Peebles. Cast: Mario Van Peebles, Stephen Baldwin, Billy Zane, Blair Underwood. Polygram, 1993

The Quick and the Dead. Director: Sam Raimi. Screenplay: Simon Moore. Cast: Sharon Stone, Gene Hackman, Leonardo Di Caprio, Russell Crowe. Tristar, 1994

Quiz Show. Director-Producer: Robert Redford. Screenplay: Paul Attanasio. Cinematography: Michael Ballhaus. Cast: Ralph Fiennes, Rob Morrow, John Turturro, Paul Scofield, David Paymer, Christopher McDonald. Buena Vista, 1994

Red River. Director: Howard Hawks. Novel *The Chisholm Trail*: Borden Chase. Cast: John Wayne, Montgomery Clift. MGM-UA, 1948

Ride the High Country. Director: Sam Peckinpah. Screenplay: NB Stone, Jr. Cast: Randolph Scott, Joel McCrea. MGM, 1962

A River Runs Through It. Director-Producer: Robert Redford. Screenplay: Richard Friedenberg. Novella: Norman Maclean. Cinematography: Philippe Rousselot. Cast: Craig Sheffer, Brad Pitt, Tom Skerritt, Emily Lloyd. Columbia, 1992.

Shane. Director: George Stevens. Screenplay: A.B. Guthrie. Novel: Jack Schaefer. Cast: Alan Ladd, Jean Arthur, Van Heflin, Jack Palance. Paramount, 1952

Sneakers. Director-Screenplay: Phil Alden Robinson. Cast: Robert Redford, Dan Aykroyd, Ben Kingsley, Mary McDonnell, River Phoenix, Sidney Poitier, David Strahairn. Universal, 1992

Spirit: Stallion of the Cimarron. Director: Kelly Asbury, Lorna Cook. Screenplay: John Fusco. Cast: Matt Damon (voice). DreamWorks, 2002

Spy Game. Director: Tony Scott. Cast: Robert Redford, Brad Pitt. Universal, 2001.

The Sting. Director: George Roy Hill. Screenplay: David Ward. Cast: Paul Newman, Robert Redford, Robert Shaw. Universal, 1973

Tell Them Willie Boy is Here. Director-Screenplay: Abraham Polonsky. Book *Willie Boy, A Desert Manhunt*: Harry Lawton. Cinematography: Conrad Hall. Cast: Robert Redford, Robert Blake, Katharine Ross. Universal, 1969

They Shoot Horses, Don't They? Director: Sydney Pollack. Novel: Horace McCoy. Cast: Jane Fonda. 20th Century Fox, 1969

This Property is Condemned. Director: Sydney Pollack. Screenplay: Francis Ford Coppola. Play: Tennessee Williams. Cast: Natalie Wood, Robert Redford. Paramount, 1966

The Treasure of the Sierra Madre. Director-Screenplay: John Huston. Cast: Humphrey Bogart, Walter Huston. Warner Bros, 1948

Three Days of the Condor. Director: Sydney Pollack. Screenplay: Lorenzo Semple, Jr., David Rayfiel. Novel *Six Days of the Condor*: James Grady. Cast: Robert Redford, Faye Dunaway. Paramount, 1975

Thunderheart. Director: Michael Apted. Screenplay: John Fusco. Cast: Val Kilmer, Sam Shepard, Graham Greene, Fred Ward, Chief Ted Thin Elk. TriStar, 1992

Tombstone. Director: George Cosmatos. Screenplay: Kevin Jarre. Cast: Kurt Russell, Val Kilmer, Sam Elliot, Dana Delaney, Michael Biehn, Bill Paxton. Hollywood Pictures, 1993.

An Unfinished Life. Director: Lasse Hallstrom Screenplay: Mark Spragg, Virginia Spragg. Novel: Mark Spragg. Cast: Robert Redford, Morgan Freeman, Jennifer Lopez, Becca Gardner, Josh Lucas. Miramax, 2005

Unforgiven. Director: Clint Eastwood. Screenplay: David Peoples. Cast: Clint Eastwood, Gene Hackman, Morgan Freeman, Richard Harris, Frances Fisher. Warner Bros, 1992

Up Close and Personal. Director: Jon Avnet. Screenplay: Joan Didion, John Gregory Dunn. Cast: Michelle Pfeiffer, Robert Redford. Touchstone, 1996

The Vanishing American. Director: George B. Seitz. Novel: Zane Grey. Cast: Richard Dix, Noha Beery, Lois Wilson. Paramount, 1925

The Virginian. Director: Victor Fleming. Novel: Owen Wister. Cast: Gary Cooper, Eugene Pallette. Paramount, 1929

War Hunt. Director: Denis Sanders. Cast: Robert Redford, Sydney Pollack, Tom Skerritt. United Artists, 1962

The Way We Were. Director: Sydney Pollack. Screenplay-Novel: Arthur Laurents. Cast: Robert Redford, Barbra Streisand. Columbia, 1973

The Westerner. Director: William Wyler. Cast: Gary Cooper, Walter Brennan. United Artists, 1940

The Wild Bunch. Director: Sam Peckinpah. Screenplay: Walon Green. Cast: William Holden, Ernest Borgnine, Robert Ryan. Warner Bros, 1969

Wild Bill. Director-Screenplay: Walter Hill. Cast: Jeff Bridges, Ellen Barkin, John Hurt, Diane Lane, David Arquette. MGM, 1995

Wyatt Earp. Director: Lawrence Kasdan. Screenplay: Dan Gordon. Cast: Kevin Costner, Dennis Quaid, Gene Hackman, Annabeth Gish, Joanna Going, Mare Winningham, Michael Madsen, Bill Pullman, Tom Sizemore. Warner Bros, 1994

Young Guns. Director: Christopher Cain. Screenplay: John Fusco. Cast: Emilio Estevez, Kiefer Sutherland, Lou Diamond Phillips, Charlie Sheen, Terence Stamp. 20th Century Fox, 1988

Young Guns II. Director: Geoff Murphy. Screenplay: John Fusco. Cast: Emilio Estevez, Kiefer Sutherland, Lou Diamond Phillips, Christian Slater. 20th Century Fox, 1990

INDEX

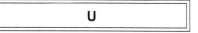

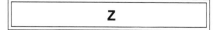

Printed in Great Britain
by Amazon